Can We Talk?

A Journey Towards Having a Healthy and Lasting Relationship

Chris Richardson

Some definitions of words are taken from Merriam–Webster's 11th Collegiate Dictionary

Edited by Yaida O. Ford
Focus Group: Corey Askew, Phillip Cummings, Dr. Pam Love Manning, Evangeline Howard
Interior layout: Jera Publishing
Photography: Jackie Hicks – www.jhicks1–FondMemories.com
Exterior Cover Design: Mandy Strong – www.mandystrong.net

Library of Congress Cataloging–in–Publication Data

Chris Richardson
Can We Talk? A Journey Towards Having a Healthy and Lasting Relationship /
Chris Richardson
p. cm.
Includes biographical references

ISBN–13: 978–1481289184
ISBN–10: 1481289187

1. Marriage – Religious Aspects – Christianity 2. Self–help – United States
Copyright © 2013 by Chris Richardson

All rights reserved.
Visit the author's website at www.RealTalkwithChrisRichardson.com.

Meaning of the Book Cover

Here you see a couple looking forward to an uncertain future. They are standing in agreement as they realize that their future possibilities are endless but risky. The pier is a strong durable structure, built to withstand against the threat of high winds and waves. For the couple, their relationship must be built on a strong durable foundation, which is Christ. As they look out into the sun setting over the hills they are reminded of the peaks and valleys of life. They know that life can sometimes take you to the edge but they are committed to endure the seasons and trials. They know that in order to live out the promise, purpose, and potential of their future together it will require Christ, communication and prayer.

Bird – Noah used a raven and a dove to determine if there was dry land after the flood. The dove represents peace, purity and the Holy Spirit. Your relationship will need the peace of God to help it endure the hard times.

Couple touching – Touching causes the brain to release a hormone called oxytocin–also known as the "love hormone." While love is more than a feeling, it is important that a couple maintains a level of physical intimacy symbolic of oneness.

Water – Water is the symbol of cleansing and is the beginning of the purification process in your acceptance with Christ. The water baptism symbolizes a spiritual rebirth that happens when one accepts Christ as Lord and Saviour.

Mountains – Mountains represent the peaks and valleys in life. Your growth in your relationship with God will determine the different spiritual levels that you will experience.

To my loving and supportive daughters, Aneya and Campbell Richardson, you continue to be the apple of my eye. I am proud of you both and I am honored to be your father and I cherish hearing you say, DADDY. To my mother Gwendolyn N. Brown, I thank you for everything that you have done and for being my bedrock over all these years. To my mentor Melanie Bonita, thank you for being obedient to the Holy Spirit and speaking life into me on Monday, April 2, 2012. Your words have forever changed the course of my life. To my childhood deacon, Frank Harvey, thank you for seeing something in me as a child that I couldn't see for myself. It is because of your words thirty years ago that I live the dream today. God is good!

Table of Contents

Foreword

You would expect a marriage therapist to write about ways to promote positive relationships amongst men and women. But an ex–Marine writing this type of book? Never in a million years! My curiosity motivated me to find out what Chris Richardson had to say about male and female relationships. Why would he be interested in the subject?

Well, this ex–Marine has a wealth of insight to share. I have deep respect for a man courageous enough to lift up the window shade to his heart and allow others to peek in on his failures. And that's exactly what you get from Chris. You experience his authenticity and transparency. You feel his passion to help couples "get it right" and honor Jesus Christ in their relationships.

Men, you will appreciate real talk and real answers from a real man. A man who can "feel you" and empathize with your concerns. Ladies, you will take a deep breath and exhale. As you read each chapter, you will say to yourself, "Finally, a man who gets me and can interpret my heart to the brothers."

My favorite parts of each chapter are the "Real Talk with Chris" moments. Metaphorically speaking, Chris goes from water skiing to scuba diving in his depth of understanding and vulnerability.

This book is a rare work from a rare man and is life changing and relationship enriching. Once you read it and use a little Vitamin A (application) you and your relationships will never be the same.

Dr. Johnny C. Parker, Jr.
Author of "Renovating Your Marriage Room by Room"

Introduction

Let me be the first to say I don't know all there is to know about relationships.

I am just as much the student as I am the author of this book. However, I wanted to share with you some of my experiences from my former marriage. Those experiences turned out to be valuable life lessons and I pray that my story will help and encourage you. I believe that along life's journey we are all tested, but if we endure, God will create a testimony. Now that I have a testimony, I want to give God glory by sharing it with you.

I was 26–years old when I got married. I just knew that when I said "I do" it was forever and truly until "death do us apart." Sadly, that was not the outcome. I never would have guessed in a million years that I would go through the trauma of a divorce. Like many others who have experienced divorce, I am not proud of having a failed marriage. I would not wish that kind of pain on my worst enemy. I was married for a total of 12–years before my divorce was finalized.

I married my ex–wife several years after serving my Country in the United States Marine Corps. I was a Marine Sergeant taught and trained how to kill a man in several ways, but not how to love a woman. I was taught how to be unemotional when dealing with the enemy, but I did not know how to be emotional when dealing with my wife. Make no mistake about it, the Marine Corps helped make me into the man that I am today. However, it was not their obligation to instill affection and compassion in my heart.

You see, that's what I lacked early on in my marriage. I was as docile as a dolphin with my wife but I did not understand emotional intimacy.

I always heard that a man shouldn't show any signs of weakness or emotional vulnerability. If I saw my wife cry I would tell her to dry her eyes and that everything would be fine. Instead, what she wanted and needed most was for me to hold her in my arms and console her. Again, I was never taught how to show affection and connect with a woman's emotions.

I grew up in a home without my biological father. My mother had to be the man and the woman of the house. She did her very best in raising me and my sister, and I am grateful for that. Unfortunately, a woman can't teach a young man how to become a man. Although I had two step–fathers, neither of them taught me the rights of passage to manhood. They did not model how a man should love, honor and appreciate his wife.

My wife and I dated several years before getting married. I was passionate and determined to prove that there were good men in this world. I even had the vanity license plate with my motto, "AFWGDMN," which stood for A Few Good Men. After I proposed to my wife, we did what all couples should do and attended premarital counseling sessions. I was certain that if we addressed certain topics during our sessions that we would be better equipped to handle life's challenges. I was wrong.

No matter how loud I said, "I do," or how much counseling we had, that did not change the outcome of our marriage. Around the 6–year mark I realized something was disconnected. Our communication was seriously lacking. I realized that it was time to get help. I thought spiritual intervention could get us back on track. I proposed to my wife that we get Christian counseling. Unfortunately, she didn't feel the same way so I went alone.

Despite the warning signs early in our relationship, we never learned to communicate our feelings, thoughts and emotions to one another in healthy ways. I saw that we were headed into a place of isolation. We were ill–prepared for what was to come. I knew we couldn't fix matters on our own. This was the part of the marriage where we didn't know what to do. Counseling was the only solution I knew.

After nagging my wife for months, I finally convinced her to go to counseling with me. She attended one or two sessions the first year and a session or two in the proceeding years. She was not committed to the idea of getting help. So every summer for the next 4–years I'd broach the subject with her about seeking counseling. Fed up with my constant prodding, she finally asked for a separation.

I turned to men's groups, church leadership and intercessory prayer (3–times per week) for moral support and spiritual guidance.

I never cheated on my wife prior to our separation, but I consumed pornography to preoccupy my mind. I concealed my porn watching and justified it because of our marital problems. I never considered the impact my new habit would have on her if she found out. Well, she found out and it only added fuel to the fires that were ravaging our marriage. Not only was I the church–going hypocrite who did the right things in public but in secret indulged his sinful desires, I was also a man who made his wife feel that she could not satisfy her husband's needs.

They say that history is the best teacher. Well, this is one history lesson that I will not repeat. It is my prayer that the words on every page that follows will permeate your heart, challenge your mind and fill your soul with the love of Christ. I challenge you to be transparent and deal with YOU before you deal with others. Too many of our children and their futures are affected by the decisions that we make today. Remember, life is choice–driven. There is never a bad time to begin making better choices.

It starts with you and ends with you. If you don't change, neither will your circumstances.

Chris Richardson

1

How's Your Relationship with God?

The book of Genesis tells the story of how God created man. From the story we learn that God formed Adam from the dust of the earth. "Then the Lord God formed a man from the dust of the ground and breathed into his nostrils the breath of life, and the man became a living being" (Genesis 2:7). Adam was the first human on earth to have a relationship with God. After God created Adam, He then created woman from Adam's rib giving him a help mate that would be suitable for him. The Lord God said, "It is not good for the man to be alone. I will make a helper suitable for him" (Gen. 2:18). We see that Adam and Eve–two whole individuals are unique and different, but they complemented each other to have a fulfilling and purposeful relationship.

In the same way God fashioned Adam and Eve, He fashioned you and me as whole beings. We do not need a man or woman to complete us. He equipped us with everything that we need to have a relationship with Him. Nevertheless, many of us go from relationship to relationship seeking validation from someone else. The chase for happiness will be elusive until you develop a healthy relationship with God. Spend time getting to know who you are in Christ. Allow God to renew your heart and mind before you decide to begin a relationship with someone else. God promises us that if we acknowledge Him, He will direct our paths. "Trust in the Lord with all your heart and lean not on your own understanding; in all your ways submit to him, and he will make your paths straight" (Proverbs 3:5–6).

A relationship with God is much like a relationship with another person only God is not subject to the same failures that we experience with men and women. When you have a relationship with God, you spend time getting to know Him by reading His Word and just talking with Him. As you develop an intimate relationship with Him, you learn to listen to His voice and trust His direction. You will still make mistakes but understand that God is building your character for His purposes and plans.

As God is molding you, you will start to realize the difference between happiness and joy. Happiness is based on our circumstances and feelings. It is here today and gone tomorrow. Joy, however, is caused by the internal awareness that God is in control no matter what is happening in your life. Joy helps you realize that He will work every situation out for your good. God wants you to have joy so that you can tell others what He has done in your life. You can only experience constant joy from an intimate relationship with God.

You may be saying, "I already know God but I still don't have the relationship with the man or woman that I want." Let me say this: to have a healthy and lasting relationship, it is imperative that we become intimate with God so He can (1) help us become the right one and (2) lead us to the right one. He wants us to know who we are in Him before we seek the companionship of others. When we give God total access to our minds, hearts and souls He will speak to us and through us. God will provide clarity for us regarding our life's purpose and ultimately our life partner.

Beloved, you must know that God will not fail you. God has promised us that if we continue to put Him first He will bless us. "But seek first his kingdom and his righteousness, and all these things will be given to you as well" (Matthew 6:33). This means that if you want to grab hold of His promises, you have to trust Him. And for you to trust Him, you have to get to know Him. When you have an intimate relationship with God, He will reveal His ways to you. Knowing God's character (e.g. His kindness, faithfulness, etc.) is important as you learn to patiently wait on Him while He brings His promises to pass in your life.

We've all heard the saying patience is a virtue. In our microwave culture, however, we want everything to happen in an instant. Those who are impatient may not experience God's plan for their lives. Because they do not spend quality time with God, they lack clear direction in their lives and often end up disappointed and disillusioned. If you have an impatient spirit ask God to help you develop patience. Patience will help you endure when times get tough and all you have to stand on is God's word.

Remember that as you get to know God, He will direct your steps. Along your journey He will guide you to the right people and places so that you can accomplish His plans for your life. This too, requires patience. God is the author and the finisher of all things. If He sets certain plans in motion, He will complete what He started if you trust and obey Him. He wants you to rely on Him and seek Him for the answers. Remember life is a journey, not a destination. Enjoy the experiences that God is giving you as you prepare for marriage or as you seek to restore a broken marriage.

If you are seeking a spouse, you should spend time praying, meditating, fasting and studying God's word. These activities will draw you closer to Him and improve your character as you seek to become a better person, and in turn, a better spouse. The best is just around the corner. If you are already married but are experiencing challenges in your relationship, start by developing an intimate relationship with God (if you have not done so already) and begin sincerely seeking Him for direction. He will order your steps and reveal His plan to you.

Real Talk with Chris

On Saturday, March 31, 2012, I connected with my true purpose for the first time. I attended a small in–home networking event and listened to several speakers talk about their businesses. One of those speakers was a young lady by the name of Melanie Bonita, who had introduced herself as an author, speaker and Daily Dose Coach. I thought to myself, "Wow! Maybe I should talk with her about what inspired her to write a book." No sooner than I engaged her in conversation did she ask me two questions that I was not prepared to answer. "What is your purpose? And what is your passion?" I paused and then responded, "I don't know." Her next question was "what are you passionate about?" Again, I paused to intently search my heart. There had to be something inside of me. After thinking about it, I blurted out "RELATIONSHIPS!" Her advice was that I pray that God clearly reveal my purpose in this area.

Two days later I spoke to her and she shared something with me that would forever change my life. She said that she had prayed for me and that God had told her that everything that I need to move forward is already within me. "It's time to give birth to it," she said. From that moment on I became laser–focused. I sought God through prayer and fasting asking Him to confirm what I believed to be my true purpose. I started journaling and began to realize the magnitude of the story within me. Before it was all said and done I had a book about relationships. Sadly, it took me 40–years to get to a point where I am finally clear about my purpose and mission in life. But I have no regrets. Now I know that God can take your pain and use it to fuel your passion.

God is Not Finished with You:

When is it good to say "no?"

When God is at work in your life, you'll have to learn how to say "no" to anyone or anything that hinders His work. To truly say "yes" to God, you must learn to remove yourself from situations that don't align with God's plan for your life.

Some of us do not like to say no but when you are striving to become a better you, learning to say no is vital. Say you have set a goal to lose 15 pounds before your class reunion in 6 months. A friend invites you over for dinner and you eat until you are full. If your friend offers you another helping, you would simply say, "no thank you" because eating when you are full creates an obstacle to your weight loss goal. Life is the same way. Sometimes you have to pass the plate that's being offered. Once you have determined to make necessary changes in your life to reach your goals, you will have to develop the ability to say NO and mean it.

 Real Talk with Chris

I have always had a difficult time saying "no" to others. I do not like saying no because I have people–pleasing tendencies. Don't get me wrong, there are some things that I can clearly say no to but I still have certain challenges. For me being a single man requires a different set of boundaries and rules than I had when I was married.

When I was married, infidelity was off the table. I had no problem saying no because I honored the covenant between me, God and my former spouse. After my divorce, it took me 18 months to get to a place where I was ready to say "yes" to God and "no" to women.

> *I got off track because of the environment that I was in, the music that I listened to and the people I was around. After realizing that my behavior was keeping me from my goal of finding real love within myself, I decided to turn my life back over to God.*

After you set your goals and begin saying no to the activities and people that will prevent you from reaching them, you must be patient and trust that God is at work in your life. Yes, it will be difficult at times but through the refining process He is transforming you into the person He wants you to become. So when you feel discouraged, remember that you are a work in progress. If you want to reap God's richest blessings in your relationships and in every area of your life, you must surrender to Him completely. Just watch out for two common pitfalls that derail us from receiving God's best–distractions and toxic relationships.

Distractions are people, places, or things that are designed to take you off course. For some of us, our family and friends can be distractions. The people who know you best can be very discouraging when you set out to make certain changes in your life. They say things like, "Why do you want to make more money?" "You'll never be able to go back to school with three kids." While I am not suggesting that you disassociate from your family members and friends, you may have to distance yourself from them or avoid discussing certain topics with them so that you can stay focused.

Scripture says that God told Moses to leave the land of his forefathers so that God could lead him to the Promised Land. "Go, assemble the elders of Israel and say to them, The Lord, the God of your fathers—the God of Abraham, Isaac and Jacob—appeared to me and said: I have watched over you and have seen what has been done to you in Egypt. And I have promised to bring you up out of your misery in Egypt into the land of the Canaanites, Hittites, Amorites, Perizzites, Hivites and Jebusites—a land flowing with milk and honey" (Exodus 3:16–17). This was major for

Moses because he had to leave everything that was comfortable and familiar if he wanted to reap God's promises. Unlike most of us though, Moses was obedient. He didn't let comfort or convenience stop him from receiving God's best. When we become disobedient, God will create a situation to get your attention. He will always let you know when certain activities or people are hindering His work in your life.

For example, say you begin contemplating whether to stop going to happy hour 2–3 nights a week. Instead, you want to join a gym and start going to bible study, but you cannot seem to decide when would be a good time to start going. One night after work you decide to go to your favorite bar. You haven't been in three weeks. When you pull up outside, you realize that the bar is closed. You text a friend who frequents the spot and he tells you that it was recently shut down for serving minors. God will send you clear signs like this to help you rid your life of distractions. This does not mean get rid of every activity in your life that is not church–related. There may also be activities at your church that God wants you to pull away from so that you can develop a closer walk with Him. Seek God for clarity as to which activities will bring you closer to fulfilling your purpose and which ones you are outside of His will for you. He will surely show you.

The other common pitfall is toxic relationships. A toxic relationship can be an abusive relationship with someone who is physically or verbally assaulting you. Another example is a relationship where one person is pulled away from their relationship with God because of their commitment to another individual. Toxic relationships are not just romantic. They can involve friends or family members, too. Do you know people who always call you to fight, cuss and fuss about anything? That person may be toxic! Everyone around you will not always have your best interest at heart. Remember, the devil comes to steal, kill and destroy (John 10:10). He wants to destroy any chance you have of fulfilling your destiny. If you ask God for discernment, wisdom and guidance regarding each individual in your circle, He will show you who needs to be there and who does not.

My son, do not forget my teaching, but keep my commands in your heart, for they will prolong your life many years and bring you peace and prosperity. Let love and faithfulness never leave you; bind them around your neck, write them on the tablet of your heart. Then you will win favor and a good name in the sight of God and man. Trust in the Lord with all your heart and lean not on your own understanding;

Proverbs 3:1–5

Once you have learned to say "no" and identify the pitfalls in your life, you must become empowered to avoid falling in those pitfalls again. God does not begin a work that He cannot finish. He wants to get you to a place where you can hear His voice and receive all that He has in store for your life. There is no formula for communicating with God but scripture reading, prayer and meditation will help you develop an intimate love relationship with God that is real and personal.

Prayer is how we speak to God by word or thought. Meditation is how you listen to God as He speaks to you. What are you petitioning God for? We often petition God for the things that we want but not for things that we need. God will never give us everything that we want, especially if it will harm us or if it is outside of His plan for our lives. Thus, our goal must be to get to a place where He is all that we need. For in this place, He will give us the desires of our heart according to His will. "Ask and it will be given to you; seek and you will find; knock and the door will be opened to you" (Matthew 7:7). If you have experienced unanswered prayers you may have given up on the practice of praying. I believe people give up on prayer because they do not know how to pray or have a misunderstanding as to what it means to pray. Prayer is two-way communication with God. You speak and then listen to what God has to say in response. Listening is where we often fall short.

If you fail to listen to God in prayer, then you will miss what He is saying to you. If you miss what He is saying to you, then you may miss what He is trying to give you. God wants to give you His best. If your desires are not in line with His will and His best for you, He may show you this through earnest prayer. However, if you are not willing to depart with your desires to do His will, then you may get what you ask for. Have you ever heard someone say, "be careful what you ask for?"

Imagine you have a favorite pair of shoes that you saved up money to buy. You absolutely love these shoes. You never see anyone else wearing them. You take good care of them, too. Later, you find out they are knock-offs of the real thing but you've grown attached to them despite the fact that you now know they are not real. Now, imagine someone very close to you asks you for your shoes. Shocked (and offended), you say "no". Why would you give up your favorite pair of shoes? Even if they are counterfeits? After thinking about it you feel bad and you give up the shoes. By this time they are worn and discolored. When you give the shoes up, the person who loves you hands you a box with a brand new pairs of shoes inside. They look similar to the shoes you first purchased but they are genuine and of better quality.

Our prayer requests can be the same way. We tell God what we want when He knows what we need. God knows what your needs are because He is omniscient, which means He knows all things. "And my God will meet all your needs according to the riches of his glory in Christ Jesus" (Philippians 4:19). I don't know about you but if I ask God for one thing and He has something better to give me, I want Him to give me what He wants me to have!

Next, we need to spend time reading the Bible. The Bible is God's word and it is a believer's instruction manual for living. If you want to know God's mind on a matter, you should look to His Word. Often, we pray about something and leave it there unsure of what to do next. After you've prayed, always look to God's word to find an answer. Remember, if you seek then you will find. He can speak to you through His Word, your pastor, another Christian friend, a radio program and so on. Just ask in faith and watch and wait for His response.

Definition of meditation. 1: a discourse intended to express its author's reflections or to guide others in contemplation. 2: the act or process of meditating. – Mirriam–Websters Dictionary

As you read God's word, meditating on it will help you apply it to your life. During meditation, God may remind you of a particular verse that you read earlier that day. Meditating on it will help you understand what God is saying to you through that verse. Or, after something wonderful happens in your life, you may pause for a moment to thank God for what He has done. This is meditating on His goodness. "But whose delight is in the law of the Lord, and who meditates on his law day and night" (Psalm 1:2). Meditation is an excellent way to strengthen your relationship with God. If you are the type of person that has a hard time sitting still, try playing soft music while you sit or journaling for 20 minutes each day.

Don't be afraid of spiritual activities. It can be intimidating to incorporate these habits into your life at first. But the rewards are overwhelming. Again, there is no formula for getting closer to God. As with any relationship, you must take the time to know Him. God is waiting. He wants to be your first love. Just find some time each day in a quiet place for the purpose of getting closer to Him. This could be your favorite room in your house, a park, near a waterfall or any place that provides tranquility. Prayer, scripture reading and meditation will enhance your ability to hear God's voice. Then you will have what you need to trust and follow His lead. Just know that God wants to speak to you and through you. He wants his light to radiate from you so that others may see His glory.

As you start removing distractions from your life and replacing them with activities that bring you closer to the One who holds your future in His hands, remember that change takes time. We move forward by taking baby steps so we don't return to old habits or toxic relationships (or new relationships that mimic the same toxic behaviors). Do not be discouraged if you are not making progress as quickly as you want. For real change to take root, you must be patient and allow God to prune you. "I am the true vine, and my Father is the gardener. He cuts off every branch in me that bears no fruit, while every branch that does bear fruit he prunes so that it will be even more fruitful. You are already clean because of the word I have spoken to you. Remain in me, as I also remain in you. No branch can bear fruit by itself; it must remain in the vine. Neither can you bear fruit unless you remain in me" (John 15:1–4). For you to be fruitful in your relationships, God must constantly prune you so that your character matches that of your life partner. God will call the two of you together to accomplish His purpose. This is major. You cannot rush the process.

Adjust Your Attitude As God Directs You

God wants His best for you but your attitude determines whether or not you will receive it. The primary difference between winners and losers is their attitude. The winner strives to be the exception and not the norm. When things get tough they work harder. They are not easily distracted. They know that all things have a season.

Change is good when your attitude is great!

Willie Jolley

Winners know that they can't quit. They understand the importance of setting goals. A goal is nothing more than a task with a deadline attached. Winners surround themselves with positive people. They are not easily discouraged. Instead of saying, "I can't" they say "I can." If you are reading this book, I hope it is because you want to win in life and in your relationships. Your new motto should become "I can do all things through Christ who strengthens me" (Philippians 4:13). Life is not a sprint; it's a marathon. When you commit to finishing a task, it's not how fast you start that matters, it's about staying the course and finishing. God will provide you with everything you need along the way to succeed. All you have to do is keep the right attitude. Here are two examples of ordinary people whose winning attitudes helped them overcome impossible circumstances.

Ana Fidelia Quirot was a world class sprinter. After suffering from third–degree burns over her hands, chest, neck, face and losing the precious life of her unborn child, many thought she would never run again. But God was not finished with Ana. He had another plan. Ana underwent 7 skin graphs and was in and out the hospital for more than 8 months. She was determined to compete again. With the help and support of her parents, treating physicians and psychologist, she was able to recover. Not long after her accident she won 2nd place with a time of 2:05.22 at the Central American and Caribbean Games in Puerto Rico an international track and field event and came close to breaking her personal record that she accomplished in the 1992 Summer Olympics. .

Born in 1951, in a small Mississippi town, Oprah Winfrey was sexually abused as a child. She attended Tennessee State University where she studied in radio and television. Oprah landed her first TV gig when she moved to Baltimore and became the host for, *"People Are Talking"*, a show which aired in 1976. Years later she was recruited by a television station in Chicago. In 1986, she launched a nationally syndicated self–titled talk show. The record–breaking Oprah Winfrey Show ran for 25 years, paved the way for scores of other talk shows and made daytime television as hot as primetime. If that wasn't enough, she launched her own magazine and television station. Although Oprah was wildly successful as a TV personality, God had other work for her to do. In January 2007, Oprah opened up her school for girls in South Africa and has led several philanthropic efforts that have changed thousands of lives.

Both of these women encountered tremendous struggles. They were ordinary people who made a choice to pursue their dreams and run with their vision. Along the journey, each of them accomplished extraordinary things. For believers, we must know that regardless of where we are in life, God is looking to use us for His glory. He can manifest your destiny just like he did in the lives of these two women. "For God does not show favoritism" (Romans 2:11).

When God is at work in your life, you have to adjust your attitude to what He is doing. You cannot have the same old mentality about life if you want to accomplish God's purpose for your life. Decide to employ an attitude that will help you soar above your circumstances. You must evict doubt, fear and discouragement from your mind. Then you must commit to taking action. Most people, when pressured by the challenges of life, give up before they reach their destination. They will never know what God had in store for them.

 # Real Talk with Chris

From the time I graduated Marine Corps boot camp in Paris Island, South Carolina, I had an unquenchable thirst for personal growth and development. I read books like "Think and Grow Rich" by Napoleon Hill and "The Greatest Miracle in the World" by Og Mandino. I listened to tapes and attended seminars to work on building my confidence and communication skills. I surrounded myself with positive people. I chose mentors who were where I wanted to be. I eliminated toxic friendships and dead—end relationships. I sought God for answers and counsel. Truthfully, I am still discovering myself and where God is taking me. Though I am clear about my purpose, life is a journey. I cannot predict the Creator's plan for my life tomorrow. One thing that I am sure of is that I can do all things through Christ who strengthens me.

Can We Talk?

Questions for you and your partner

The following questions will allow you to assess where you are on your journey to oneness with your spouse and God.

1. Do you believe in God?

   ☐ Yes   ☐ No

2. How would you describe your relationship with God? How's your relationship with yourself?

   _____

   _____

   _____

3. Do you pray?

   ☐ Yes   ☐ No

4. How often do you pray?

   _____

5. Do you meditate?

   ☐ Yes   ☐ No

6. How often do you meditate?

   _____

7. What are the distractions in your life?

   _____

   _____

   _____

8. What are the toxic relationships that you need to eliminate?

_____

_____

_____

9. Who or what is it hard for you to say no to?

_____

_____

_____

10. What is God's purpose for your life?

_____

_____

_____

11. What about your attitude could you change? What would your clos-
    est family members and friends say?

_____

_____

_____

12. What have you given up on too soon?

_____

_____

_____

13. What is your passion?

_____

_____

_____

14. What is your vision for your life?

_____

_____

_____

Notes:

_____

_____

_____

_____

_____

2

The To–do's You Do
Before Saying "I Do"

There are several things that every man and woman
should do to prepare themselves for marriage. I advise you and your potential mate to discuss what
marriage means to you and your expectations of one another. But before you do that, be honest with yourself as
to why you are getting married. Make a list of the pros
and cons. Marriage is for mature adults. Thus, the decision should be made carefully and prayerfully. The following tips will help you think through issues that you
want to discuss before you get married.

To-do #1:

Stop Fantasizing and Start Examining

All too often we fantasize about what our happy marriage will look like instead of examining what it takes to get there. I call this "The Cinderella Syndrome." Once upon a time a long time ago there lived a little girl named Cinderella. Cinderella was a very unhappy little girl. She lost her mother and her father remarried before she had time to grieve. Cinderella did not like her father's selection. We all know the rest of the story.

A number of women dream of being the modern day Cinderella. They dream of meeting their prince charming, donning a beautiful dress on their wedding day and living happily ever after,. For some women, the quest to become Cinderella never ends. They look for the man to marry and want to live happily ever after but do not anticipate the hard work of getting to "happily ever after." They soon learn that a strong marriage takes work that they did not prepare to do.

In many instances the preparation for the wedding far exceeds the planning for after the wedding. The planning phase is carefully detailed. All of the pieces of the wedding ceremony must be laid out like a 200 piece jigsaw puzzle. There has to be a wedding coordinator, a perfect venue, a perfect day and time, perfect announcements, perfect programs, perfect order of the ceremony, perfect brides maids, perfect grooms men, perfect cake, perfect colors, perfect theme, perfect guest list, and the list goes on.

Marriage is not a fairytale and we must thoroughly examine life after the wedding. Most couples spend more time planning the big day rather than working on sustaining their vows. They forget that it requires work to have a thriving marriage. So shortly after the vows are exchanged, reality sinks in and couples realize that marriage is not easy. A strong marriage requires prayer, focus, determination, commitment, humility, transparency, vulnerability, truthfulness and so much more. Remember, marriage is for mature adults. Not everyone is ready to put in the work it takes to reach happily ever after.

Real Talk with Chris

*I*s the Cinderella story just for girls? I don't think so. When I was a child, I dreamt about the day when I would ask for a young woman's hand in matrimony. Although my parents and grandparents did not model the type of marriage that I hoped for, I still desired to become a husband. My grandfather and grandmother were married until the day my grandfather passed away. They were from Kyle, West Virginia. They were both very strong willed and determined. My grandmother was a church going woman that would give you the shirt off of her back. My grandfather was a man's man, strong in his convictions and beliefs. He loved to listen to baseball on the radio and sit around and read the Sunday paper. However, as a child I never witnessed him hugging or kissing my grandmother. I noticed that when they went to bed at night they slept in separate rooms. As a child, this was something that I could never fully understand.

My mother's marriages were different. She was married three times. Although, I never experienced what it was like to have my father in my life, I can tell you what it was like to live without him. My experience growing up as a child was similar to Cinderella's. I had two step—fathers and, while one of them was a father—figure to me, neither of them modeled how a godly man treats his wife. In hindsight, I wish that my mother had married the type of man who followed Christ with all his heart and loved her, the way Christ loved the church. That is the type of model I wished I'd had.

When I initially got married, I was certain that my marriage would not be like those modeled for me. I was willing to work twice

> as hard to see it through. However, I did not allow God to choose the
> right one for me. One of the greatest challenges for me and a number of
> men is marrying the person that God has chosen for us versus the one
> we have chosen for ourselves. "But the Lord said to Samuel, "Do not
> consider his appearance or his height, for I have rejected him. The Lord
> does not look at the things people look at. People look at the outward
> appearance, but the Lord looks at the heart" (1 Samuel 16:7). All too
> often, we marry the person who seems to be the right person during a
> particular season in our lives. God chooses the one who is right for the
> entirety of our lives. Unfortunately, some don't realize that the shoe
> doesn't fit until it's too late.

To-do #2:
Identify God's Plan for Your Life

God is the originator of all things. In the beginning, God chose Eve for
Adam. Before you say, "I do," it is critical that you spend time seeking God
for confirmation of His plan for you. Selecting your mate is a life–altering decision. If you choose poorly, it will impact your life and the lives of
others. Thus, you want to seek God for His plan for your life before you
marry. This way you will be more conscientious about selecting a partner
who is also seeking God's plan for their life.

If you are not married yet, this is definitely the time that you want to
spend earnestly seeking God. You want to ask God to order your steps
and guide your heart. As He speaks to you, it is important that you listen
to His voice and obey what He says. You also want to pray that God reveal, uncover and remove any distractions that are not part of His plan.

Many people are unsure how to hear from God. These people often
go through life with the mindset that if it does not work out then it is

not meant to be. They experience disappointment after disappointment in their relationships and hurt others in the process. This can be avoided by taking time to cultivate an intimate relationship with God so He can direct you (see chapter 1). Prayer, alone, is not enough to confirm what God may be saying to you about your potential mate. Our hearts can lead us astray, especially in the areas of love and marriage. "The heart is deceitful above all things and beyond cure. Who can understand it?" (Jeremiah 17:9). This is why you must ask God to confirm what you believe He said to you in prayer.

When you ask God for confirmation, wait until He responds before you decide in your heart that you have received an answer. Waiting is not passive; it is actively anticipating what God is about to do. While you wait, have faith that God will respond clearly to your requests. "And without faith it is impossible to please God, because anyone who comes to him must believe that he exists and that he rewards those who earnestly seek him" (Hebrews 11:6). God will honor His Word but you must do your part. Ask Him to send you godly people to pray with you during this period. Keep your ears open for messages that you may hear in church or while riding in your car or on the train. God will speak to you but you must posture your heart to receive His answer.

For many of us, instead of waiting on God to confirm His plan and partner for our lives, we get caught up in the euphoria of a new romance. When this happens, we often fail to hear God speak. We miss the obvious signs and patterns that He reveals to us about the other person's character. Beloved, you must realize that not everyone is ready and willing to handle the responsibilities that come with marriage. This could be you. Don't say "I do" if you don't. You can't afford to let your flesh lead you in making such a vital decision. "For if you live according to the flesh, you will die; but if by the Spirit you put to death the misdeeds of the body, you will live" (Romans 8:13). There's too much at stake. Your life and legacy depend on the decisions that you make today. When you ask God to order your steps, you have to submit your fleshly desires to Him so that you can make the right decision about which relationship to pursue. This is all a part of identifying God's plan for your life.

Your spouse is the person who will be connected to you and everything that you do for a lifetime. This is the person with whom you've exchanged vows agreeing to support each other in the good times and the bad times. Your spouse is the person with whom you will share your dreams, visions and goals. Your spouse is the person who will parent your children and be responsible for guarding your inner most secrets. Thus, you must consult God first. Ideally, before you select your spouse you would already have a committed relationship with God. If not, start today. It is never too late to accept Christ as your Lord and Savior, repent of your past sins and ask Him to show you His plan for your life.

To–do #3:
Find Someone who is Equally Yoked

God wants you to be equally yoked and connected to the right person. Just because she goes to church one Sunday out of the month doesn't make her equally yoked. Similarly, just because he listens to the gospel station in the car and has Joel Osteen books sitting on the coffee table doesn't make him a godly man. God's word tells us that it is important to be involved with someone of the same faith. "Do not be yoked together with unbelievers. For what do righteousness and wickedness have in common? Or what fellowship can light have with darkness?" (2 Corinthians 6:14).

If you are patient and allow God to lead you He will reveal your partner to you. Ladies, just because he says he prays for you, doesn't mean he is your husband. Men are hunters by nature so be wary of men who use prayer as a tool to make themselves look spiritual when there is no other proof of a life committed to God. Fellas, don't get too caught up with her looks because beauty is only skin deep. Remember Forrest Gump? My man Forrest understood this principle so well that he coined his own phrase, "Pretty is as pretty does." If she's pretty on the outside but ugly on the inside, she's pretty ugly. Ladies, this is also applicable to men.

Just because you meet someone with potential does not mean they are equally yoked with you. Take time to hear from God and get to know the person long enough to discern their motives. Everyone can fake it for a short period of time but the truth will always emerge. In the meantime, find out the other person's views on spirituality. Ask them questions about their relationship with God. If they shy away from the subject or say that it's private then more than likely they are not equally yoked with you. Keep both eyes open and ask the right questions because your future depends on it.

To-do #4:

Learn How to Appreciate Your Differences

Ladies, you can't CHANGE him, only God can. Fellas, never look at a potential mate as a "project." What you see is what you get. From the time you were born, God made you unique and different. Within your marriage you must learn how to appreciate your spouse for their differences. If not you will always try to change them to think the way you think and act the way you act. Remember, men and women were meant to complement one another.

You may not always share the same opinion with your spouse, but you must learn how to respect each other and appreciate the different experiences and perspectives you each bring to the table. It is important that you understand and discuss this in the very beginning. Often, your partner's views and opinions are based on experiences they had as a child. Take time to talk about your families and childhoods. I am not saying you will learn all there is to know about your partner, but when you start to question certain behaviors he or she exhibits, knowing some of their past experiences will help you develop a more accepting attitude.

When situations arise during your marriage you and your spouse may respond to them in a totally different manner. It is very important that you learn how to embrace this principle early on. Realize that your partner may not always see things your way. Do not insult your partner's opinion. This will inhibit open communication in your relationship. Be careful not to criticize, tear down or personally attack your partner. Instead, establish basic rules of engagement in the beginning and make sure that you follow them.

Always think before you speak. Be an active listener and make sure you understand what your partner is saying before you respond. Try listening with your heart and not with your mouth. Then think about your response and how it will be perceived. Before you respond, ask yourself, "How can I encourage an open dialogue?" If you are angry or your partner is angry, think about the timing of your response. Rather than responding right away, it may be best to wait.

My favorite TV couple is Cliff and Claire Huxtable. They did not always see eye–to–eye on things but they valued each others' opinion. They knew when to speak up and they knew when to retreat to their respective corners. As husband and wife your future depends on your ability to appreciate your differences. If every petty disagreement turns into World War III, then you are headed for trouble. Many eyes are watching how you relate to each other, including your children. Remember you cannot change your spouse. Decide how you will handle major disagreements and stick to the plan as much as possible.

To–do #5:

Read and Discuss Your Marriage Vows Together

A good time to discuss the vows is before saying "I do," not afterwards. Many people go through the ceremony and exchange the vows, but haven't discussed what these vows really mean to each other. Suppose your partner has an issue or a different view on the words. It's best to discuss this early on rather than go through the motions and not address it at all.

At the altar the minister stands at the front in the center of the couple asking each party to repeat the following: *will you have this man/woman as thy wedded husband/wife, to live together after God's ordinance in the holy estate of matrimony? Will you love him/her, comfort him/her, honor, and keep him/her in sickness and in health; and, forsaking all others, keep thee only unto him/her, so long as you both live?*

These vows are deep and many people utter them and do not give them a second thought. Beloved, you must take these vows seriously. You are not only repeating them before your friends and family, you are repeating them before the Almighty God. This may seem like a pointless exercise, but read the vows first and then meditate on their meaning. If you still feel like reading the vows is a waste of time after this, then perhaps you are not ready to exchange them.

To-do #6:

Take God with You... Don't Leave Him at the Altar

If you're already unhappy in your relationship, getting married won't resolve your problems. Only God can. It is critical that you understand that God is the glue that keeps the relationship in tact. All too often we ask God to bless our marriage but then we leave Him at the altar. According to God's word, marriage is a blood covenant that is meant to be upheld unto death. The Marriage covenant is between three people–a man, a woman and God. Contracts can be broken but not covenants. If you do not realize this, you will not have the proper perspective you need when problems arise in your marriage.

For a marriage to survive it must be planted in the proper soil. A relationship is healthiest when two people are rooted in God. If both husband and wife keep Him at the center, they will have a fruitful marriage.

"Remain in me, as I also remain in you. No branch can bear fruit by itself; it must remain in the vine. Neither can you bear fruit unless you remain in me. I am the vine; you are the branches. If you remain in me and I in you, you will bear much fruit; apart from me you can do nothing" (John 15:4–5).

If you want a successful relationship, faith in God cannot be an option. Trials, tests and tribulations will come but if you are both connected to the same source (God), you will overcome and your relationship will be strengthened.

Can We Talk?

Questions for you and your partner

The following questions will allow you to assess where you are on your journey to oneness with your spouse and God.

1. What's your perspective on marriage? What does a thriving marriage look like?

   _____

   _____

   _____

2. What are your expectations for yourself and your spouse in marriage?

   _____

   _____

   _____

3. In what areas of your relationship with your spouse or partner do you experience the greatest difficulty?

   _____

   _____

   _____

4. What differences do you appreciate about your spouse or partner?

   _____

   _____

   _____

5. What do the vows mean to you? What would you change in the vows? Why?

_____

_____

_____

6. Why is it important to you that God be in our relationship? Why can't we leave Him at the altar?

_____

_____

_____

Notes:

_____

_____

_____

_____

_____

3

What is LOVE?

Is love a feeling? A thought? An action? Scripture characterizes love as all of the above. "Love is patient, love is kind. It does not envy, it does not boast, it is not proud. It is not rude, it is not self–seeking, it is not easily angered, it keeps no record of wrongs. Love does not delight in evil but rejoices with the truth. It always protects, always trusts, always hopes, and always perseveres" (1 Corinthians 13:4–7).

We know what love is supposed to look like, but there are different types of love that we express to those with whom we have relationships. We love our friends, spouses, children and others but not with the exact same type of love. As you review the list of love types below, try to match the different types of love with your various relationships past or present.

Real Talk with Chris

I didn't know what love was supposed to look like before I got married. Growing up as a child the examples that I had before me did not model the behaviors of love. I did not have a monogamous relationship with Christ to help me understand how valuable my role would be as a husband. I didn't know how to spell celibacy much less practice it. The bottom line is that I did not know what it meant to love myself before I tried to love someone else. You see, my perception of love was molded by my past experiences. I didn't know my marriage would have the same outcome as the marriages I'd witnessed growing up. I have accepted responsibility for my choices, but I now understand that my family history effected my future decisions. I made poor choices. I spent more time acting on my flesh and pursuing love in all the wrong places than I did pursuing God's love and plan for my life. I didn't know what love was or how to love. I spent time pursuing a feeling. So let me ask you, what is love?

This can be a very helpful exercise, but get ready. The truth hurts but it can also set you free.

The Different Types of Love

Storge

This type of love is between parents and children. It is also very common amongst friends and family. Even after lover's part ways, this type of love can be found in the form of friendship.

Mania

This type of love is a very obsessive and volatile form of love and is most common among people with low self–esteem. It can manifest as jealousy and possessiveness. This type of love can be very dangerous.

Ludus

This type of love is a mirage of love but it is not the real thing. The lover just wants to have fun without any strings attached. They are not looking for love with any level of intimacy or intensity.

Eros

This type of love is emotional and physical. Eros is commonly known as the sexual love. God's word instructs us that this type of love is for a man and his wife. It can go beyond sexual parameters, but it is motivated by selfishness. It is not concerned about the other person and is based on attraction and desire. The Eros type of love fades away with time.

Pragma

This is a practical type of love with realistic needs and can sometimes be unemotional. A person who is pragmatic in their relationships usually seeks a partner that has a basic set of qualities that suits a particular need in their life.

Phileo

This type of love is referred to as brotherly love in the Bible. This is a deep–rooted emotion where love grows and both partners are benefiting from the friendship. Phileo love goes beyond superficial needs in a relationship leaving the desire to strive for a deeper connection.

Agape

This type of love is most common in the Bible. Christ loved the Church with Agape love. He served willingly and selflessly. In a marriage, this type of love is the most enduring. Many people jump into relationships for different reasons. There are some that go from relationship to relationship trying to find love. They are in love with being in love. They always need the security and comfort of being with someone. Beloved, you have to love yourself first before you can offer love to someone else. It's impossible for you to give what you don't have.

Love Distorted

You might have been verbally or physically abused in your last relationship. You might have been unappreciated and undervalued. You may feel like you are trapped inside of a box because they said they love you but their actions don't show it. Ladies, don't be tricked by his attempt to say, "I love you" after he has verbally or physically abused you. You are not a garbage can or a punching bag. Don't mistake abuse, rage, envy or his jealousy for love.

Some women and men confuse what is merely good sex with love. Love is more than just good sex. Dogs have sex with other dogs all the time. After they finish they go about their business as if nothing ever happened. They don't stick around and try to convince each that they are in love. Be careful, if you put sex into the relationship early on it is a recipe for trouble. Ladies, if you want him to stick around for the main entree stop advertising and enticing him with the dessert. Stop sending him mixed signals. There's an appropriate place and time for you to reveal your goodies. He won't look at you in a godly way if you are massaging his imagination before stimulating his intellect. The key to a man's heart is through his mind not his eyes.

Sex is every man's battle. Don't be fooled by his smoothness and sophistication. There are several challenges with getting physical too soon. First, you miss warning signs about the other person's character because sex distorts your perspective. Second, if the relationship fails you feel guilty that you were not more guarded. Finally, the promise, purpose and potential the relationship could have had may never be realized.

Not only is sex before marriage outside God's plan, but you will open up Pandora's Box of he-motions and she-motions that will guide your decisions rather than God's voice. Once sex is in the picture, the chemistry and the dynamics of the relationship will change. You've created a soul tie without the union of marriage. A soul tie is where two people's souls connect through the act of sex. This causes challenges, especially if the relationship doesn't work out because each of you have taken a piece of that person with you to the next relationship without even realizing it. Sex has the power to influence your thoughts and emotions. Ultimately, you give away that power when you have sex prematurely. Now, instead of God ordering your steps, you have given your flesh that authority. Considering how crazy our flesh is, the thought of it ruling our relationships is scary.

When it comes to the expression of love, women need a reason and season. Most women want to feel connected with their partner before having sex. Many women value themselves and respect their bodies more than to just lie down and go through the motions of having sex without an emotional connection. Men on the other hand don't need a reason. They don't need a connection. They just need a place (e.g. car, countertop, garage, etc.). To him, it's just sex. Ladies, having sex with a man before marriage will not give him an emotional connection to you. However, when you are married a man will want sex to bond emotionally with you.

Men need to release their feelings and women like to show their feelings. In other words, a man won't express his emotions like a woman does. Men tend to keep their emotions bottled inside. However, he will express his love and emotions through the act of sex. This is how he releases his emotions. Comparatively, a woman likes to show her feelings and emotions through her expressions and actions outside of the bedroom. Now, for a man, he will show and express true love for her beyond the bedroom if he believes she is "the one." This is where men differ from women.

So ladies, if he hasn't said, "I love you." Does he? In this case, do his words speak louder than his actions? Don't miss the obvious signs and confuse LUST for LOVE. Lust is self-centered and all about filling your sexual appetite and desires of the flesh. Love focuses on the other person's needs. If you are single, don't give away your power. Hold it until your honeymoon.

If you are married and you want your partner to not only show you but tell you that he loves you, you need to show him how that looks. Men are very visual. Don't just give him clues, show him and tell him how you feel when he does special things that you really like. Flattery to a man's ego will take you a long way. Reward and celebrate his behavior. Take time to talk about what pleasing you looks like without emasculating him.

Be open, real and honest with yourself and share with him what you need. Once you've shown him, reinforce the behavior when he does it. Remember, men and women are completely different. Nothing can be implied when it comes to us men. In other words, don't assume that over time he should naturally do what pleases you. Behavioral changes require time and constant reinforcement. Be patient and willing to teach him.

> *Husbands, love your wives, just as Christ loved the church and gave himself up for her to make her holy, cleansing her by the washing with water through the word, and to present her to himself as a radiant church, without stain or wrinkle or any other blemish, but holy and blameless. In this same way, husbands ought to love their wives as their own bodies. He who loves his wife loves himself.*
>
> Ephesians 5:25–28

Most of all, keep communication open. You should discuss your expectations on an ongoing basis. But remember the best example of what LOVE is was the example that Christ modeled for man. He showed love through His actions and His words. Your husband is not Christ, but hopefully he is striving to be Christ–like each day.

Love Her Like Christ Loved the Church

Now that she has taught you what loves looks like to her, love her as Christ loved the church.

During His tenure here on earth Christ made an impact on everyone He came into contact with and beyond. Christ led by example for His disciples and for the world. He taught us what service should look like and what unconditional love means. But most importantly, He taught us, as men, how to prioritize our affection. For Christ, the church was His number one priority.

When you are married, God wants you to know that your first ministry is to serve your wife and your family like Christ served the church.

The same way Christ prayed for strength to do God's will on earth, God wants you to seek Him for help and strength to love and to lead your wife. He wants you to pour into her like Christ poured into the church. As a husband, you are required by scripture to love your wife as you love yourself. To love yourself you've got to know who you are in Christ. If you love yourself you can love your wife without putting your hands on her. You can love her without wishing her ill. You can love her by speaking life into her.

A woman doesn't mind following you as long as you know where you're going. Have a plan. You've tried it your way, now try God's. Don't know how to get a plan? Do what Christ did. He communicated with God on a regular basis, received instructions and fulfilled God's plan for His life. He ministered, taught, served and healed and ultimately died for others. Let your actions mirror Christ's as you serve your wife. No pressure. No one is perfect but if you seek God first, He will empower you to fulfill your role as a husband, father, author, gardener, pastor or whatever He has purposed for you.

Honor and Respect Him like the Church Honors and Respects Christ

"Wives, submit yourselves to your own husbands as you do to the Lord. For the husband is the head of the wife as Christ is the head of the church, his body, of which he is the Savior. Now as the church submits to Christ, so also wives should submit to their husbands in everything" (Ephesians 5:22–24). Since His birth, Jesus has been one of the most revered, honored and respected individuals ever to walk this earth. The church has continued to honor Him since His death and resurrection.

Let everyone be subject to the governing authorities, for there is no authority except that which God has established. The authorities that exist have been established by God. Consequently, whoever rebels against the authority is rebelling against what God has instituted, and those who do so will bring judgment on themselves.

Romans 13:1–2

Just as God made Christ the head of the church, God requires order and accountability in marriage. Christ was married to the church. He was accountable for His actions and He led by example. Similarly, the husband's role is to lead his wife and their family. The wife's role is to honor and respect him like the church honors and respects Christ. God is requiring that we have order in everything that we do. We must always respect God–ordained roles. We see this requirement in scripture.

Ladies, God is holding you accountable for your actions. It is important to know that God rewards those who diligently seek him. Honor God's word by honoring and respecting the position your husband plays in your household. I know it might be hard when you disagree with his decisions but remember, your ultimate goal is to please God. You may not realize this, but how you treat your husband matters to God. When it is all said and done the words that you want to hear are, "Well done, *thou* good and faithful servant"

Teach Me How to LOVE

Love is a universal language. People write songs about it, make movies about it, fight about it and the list goes on. No matter who you are or where you are from, you want to be loved by someone. The problem is our culture's view of love is so distorted that none of us knows what real love looks like and this has an impact on the way we relate to one another. Let me break it down even further.

Ladies, most men don't know how to LOVE you. He may want to show you his heart and open up but he really doesn't know how. He wants to bring down the walls but he doesn't know how to quiet his pride. You have to be willing to be patient and show him how you want to be loved. You have to teach him what love is and what love means to you. Don't nag him but encourage him throughout the teaching process. He wants to learn how to hear your heart, not your mouth. Try reading a book together like "The 5 Love Languages" by Gary Chapman. Talk to each other about what LOVE looks like to each of you. You both want the same thing. Everyone wants to feel loved, valued, appreciated, honored and respected. Men and women just say it in a different language.

Maybe you've heard the saying "you can catch more flies with honey, than with vinegar." If you're already frustrated, angry and bitter you won't get his attention. The energy that you are giving him is toxic and he can feel all of that. Men are like thermometers so when the temperature in a relationship changes, we know it. Your actions always speak louder than your words.

When a man expresses his feelings and shows affection he is essentially saying, "I trust you." He is letting you into his heart. Most men don't want to be vulnerable and are afraid of rejection. He doesn't want to feel that he has lost control. For the man that chooses to let down his guard he is opening the doors to his castle. He is shedding layers of this tough and rugged exterior. He is showing you that he is willing to allow you into his inner sanctuary. One of the most important things to embrace early on in your relationship is to remember that you both hold each others hearts in your hands. The heart is very sensitive and you both must remember to hold it ever so gently, be kind to it, cherish it and most importantly, LOVE it.

Fellas, if your lady is pouring in to you, it's only right that you go above and beyond to sow back into her. Remember, you reap what you sow. "Do not be deceived: God cannot be mocked. A man reaps what he sows" (Galatians 6:7–9). If she wants you to spend time with her, then do it. Eliminate the distractions. Turn off the TV and the cell phone. Just listen to her. When she is sharing something with you, she's not always looking for you to solve the problem or provide a solution. Sometimes, she just wants to confide in you.

If your spouse needs or wants compliments, what are you waiting for? Do you want them to ask you each time they feel you should say something nice to them? That's ridiculous. Think about it this way. When someone comes into your life they can either add value or take it away. Maybe, as a result of your relationship with your partner you have become a better person today. Show them. If he likes small gifts now and then, get them. Give her flowers unexpectedly. It's better to show love while you have a chance.

 Can We Talk?

Questions for you and your partner

The following questions will allow you to assess where you are on your journey to oneness with your spouse and God.

1. What is your definition of love?

    _____

    _____

    _____

2. What is your love language? What is your spouses love language?

    _____

    _____

    _____

3. How do you respond to love?

    _____

    _____

    _____

4. How do you show your love to your spouse?

    _____

    _____

    _____

5. Now that you know your spouses love language what can you do differently?

    _____

    _____

    _____

6. What did you learn from this chapter?

_____

_____

_____

Notes:

_____

_____

_____

_____

_____

4

Service with a Smile

Can you remember the best restaurant experience you've ever had? What made that experience so great for you? Was it the food? Was it the ambiance you felt when you walked through the door? Was it your server? Now, think about the worst restaurant experience you've had. I bet you remember your bad experience more vividly than you do your great experience. This is why great restaurants focus on service as much as they do food. Service is everything. If you want to have a successful relationship, you must internalize this principle. Serve your mate with no other motive but to make his or her day. And if you really want to hit a homerun, serve him with a smile on your face (or at least wipe the mean mug off and take your hands off your hips while doing it).

I know it's hard. Serving unconditionally requires sacrifice. If it is easy for you to do all day, every day, then it is not a sacrifice. If it does not interfere with the football game or your favorite reality TV show, it is not a sacrifice. If it takes time away from something that is important to you, it is a sacrifice. If it is something that you do not feel like doing but you will just to see the look on your mate's face, it is a sacrifice. It's not always about YOU. Ask any happy couple that has survived the test of time, they'll tell you that along the way they made sacrifices. If this concept is hard for you to grasp, try changing your perspective. Don't look at service as a form of "slavery." You have to see it as a labor of love.

Christ is the ultimate example of service. In serving His disciples and the people, He showed others how to serve selflessly. "For even the Son of Man did not come to be served, but to serve, and to give his life as a ransom for many" (Mark 10:45). You might be thinking, "Chris, I'm not Jesus. Have you seen my wife's attitude?" Or if you're a wife you may be saying, "He may say 'thank you' but he doesn't really appreciate anything that I do for him." Beloved, to serve like Christ you must be willing to die to your flesh. This means that you will follow His example even when you don't want to. What sacrifices have you made lately? In your relationship, have you shown your partner that you will serve him or her with a Christ-like attitude?

If serving like Christ is too daunting a comparison for you, think about it in terms of the 5:1 rule. Tom Rath and Donald O. Clifton wrote a book titled, "How Full Is Your Bucket?" The book is about how positive interactions and reinforcement with others can boost productivity. In a relationship, one of the best ways to make your partner feel more appreciated is by making a daily deposit into their bucket five times per day. In return, you withdraw from their bucket once per day.

In a relationship there are four buckets: emotional, intellectual, physical and spiritual. The goal is to serve your partner unselfishly by applying the 5:1 rule in these areas. Applying this rule helps reinforce positive behaviors and cultivates a healthier relationship. If doing five nice things for your spouse in a 24-hour period is still too daunting for you, then start by doing one nice thing each day. You will notice a difference in your partner's behavior. For example, surprise them by leaving a nice card for them to read at the breakfast table. Pack their lunch. Surprise them by telling them that you will pick up the kids from school today. Give them a day of rest and relaxation away from their daily duties. These are just some of the things that you can do to make daily deposits into their buckets. Remember, great service requires great sacrifice.

Ask yourself, "How would my relationship change if I sincerely served my partner?" Imagine the ways your relationship will improve by you serving your partner with a willing heart. Christ served people He did not even know and He did it from the heart. How can we not do the same for the people with whom we are the most intimate? God wants us to serve our spouses. I'm not saying your spouse is your servant. Just because he or she cooks dinner doesn't make them so. Servants work out of obligation. Spouses serve out of love. Discuss the possibilities of taking turns with some of the daily household responsibilities. Show them through your acts of service how much you care for them and love them.

How You Serve Matters

Let's revisit our favorable restaurant experience. I like an attentive server. He or she addresses the *little things* right away and without me having to ask. Those *little things* seem small but are very important. I make judgments about a place from the time I walk through the door. If I feel ignored when I walk in, I am already under the impression that I will get bad service.

Similarly, in every relationship it's the small things that make a huge difference. Ignoring the little things that make your partner happy (saying "thank you" or "good morning") will add up and create challenges. Talk to your partner about the level of service you want and be prepared to hear what they want too. Having this conversation early on can help you set the stage for a healthy, lasting relationship.

In your relationships with one another, have the same mindset as Christ Jesus: Who, being in very nature God, did not consider equality with God something to be used to his own advantage; rather, he made himself nothing by taking the very nature of a servant, being made in human likeness. And being found in appearance as a man, he humbled himself by becoming obedient to death— even death on a cross!

Philippians 2:5–8

You may have heard of the golden rule or the platinum rule. The golden rule is commonly known as "treat others the way you want to be treated." The platinum rule is "Treat others the way they want to be treated." I like the platinum rule. The way you and I want to be treated could be different. Thus, it makes sense to serve your spouse the way that they want to be served versus the way you would want someone to serve you.

Just like a good server you've got to pay attention to the details. How you serve really matters. Ladies, if you serve selfishly and begrudgingly he can immediately pick up on that. If you are putting up a front and doing things out of obligation, your actions will create unnecessary tension within the relationship. Fellas, remember you reap what you sow. Don't take your problems from work home with you and take it out on your spouse. Your wife is there for your support but don't expect her to be a dumping ground for all the drama and negativity you dealt with throughout the day. Then expect her to turn around and be ready to serve you with a smile. It's just not gonna happen.

If you've had a rough day at work or school or home with the kids, take time to gather yourself before you start interacting with your spouse. This will ensure that the two of you get off on the right foot after a long day. Tell your spouse before you settle down for the evening that you need a moment to deprogram from your day. Remember, you're still a husband or wife regardless of what happens outside of your home. Instead of coming through the door without speaking, try embracing your spouse with a 10 second kiss and affectionate embrace. Let them hear the words, "I love you and missed you." Do the same with your kids. And then take a minute to get yourself together and shake off whatever frustrations, fears or doubts had you wrapped up all day. Now you can effectively serve your family.

As men, when we are dealing with things we do not want to share with our wives, we tend to go into isolation. Again, it's not about YOU. Consider the feelings of your wife and children. How does that make them feel to see daddy come through the doors without giving them a proper greeting or any quality time? What kind of example are you setting for your wife and children? Is this the behavior that you want them to model?

We have a duty to love our families. It can be difficult to do at times, but regardless of how we feel, it is our responsibility to show care and concern for our wives and children. How do you feel when you know you are coming home to a family who is eager to see you? When you come home your wife and kids are reading your body language and watching your every expression. Your attitude sets the tone for the entire household. Speak life into your household. You can change your desired outcome by controlling your thoughts and correcting your actions. Simply take a deep breath and visualize positive thoughts of interacting with your family before you walk through the door.

Remember, words are containers of power. What you say (or don't say) will make or break your relationships. "The tongue has the power of life and death, and those who love it will eat its fruit" (Proverbs 18:21). Watch what you say. Christ told religious leaders that what comes out of a man's mouth is more important than what he puts in it (Matthew 15:18). Many of us believe that as long as we say something good about our spouse it will balance out all the negative things we say. Wrong! "Out of the same mouth come praise and cursing. My brothers and sisters, this should not be" (James 3:10).

6 Key Ingredients to Serving Your Partner

Here are six key ingredients that can help you close the communication gap in your relationship. Use these ingredients every day and watch things change for the better.

1. **Apply the 5:1 rule.** Make five deposits to one withdrawal in your partner's buckets every day.

2. **Serve unconditionally.** Serve them whether you feel like it or not. No strings attached.

3. **Make the small things more important.** If it matters to your partner then it should matter to you.

4. **Be attentive to their needs.** Take the initiative. Ask them if they need help.

5. **Serve continuously.** After you've served them check on them again just like a good server.

6. **Apply the Platinum Rule.** Treat your spouse the way he or she wants to be treated.

How Do I Serve When I Don't Feel Like Serving?

The ultimate act of service was Christ's death on the cross for us. While He lived, He exemplified what service is all about. You and I can never become Christ but we can choose to become more like Him. If this is your goal, start at home with your family. Next time you don't feel like serving, ask yourself the question, "Am I truly committed to becoming more like Christ?" Then remind yourself what Christ did for mankind. This will help you serve when you do not want to. You are not serving only to please your spouse; you are serving because you want to be more like Christ. "Whatever you do, work at it with all your heart, as working for the Lord, not for human masters, since you know that you will receive an inheritance from the Lord as a reward. It is the Lord Christ you are serving" (Colossians 3:23–24).

After that, he poured water into a basin and began to wash his disciples' feet, drying them with the towel that was wrapped around him.

John 13:5

There are consequences for not providing good service. Most servers make the majority of their money in tips. If a server isn't at their best they know there is a strong likelihood that they may not receive a good tip, if they receive one at all. Just like a server at a restaurant, there's a price to pay for not giving your mate your best. When a server has a bad day and is not at their best it doesn't change their guests' expectations. Their guests are still looking for good food and great service. Similarly, your spouse still expects you to treat them with love and respect even when you are having a bad day. You get out of a relationship what you put into it. Remember the 5:1 rule.

For example, you want to go out to dinner but your husband is asking you for a little time to relax and unwind in the man cave tonight and suggests having dinner out tomorrow night. (*Side bar: Man cave – Typically known as the get–away location in the home as designated by your husband; most commonly found in the basement.*) He has been working on several projects on and off the job, which have been extremely time–consuming. He just needs some time to himself to think, relax, and clear his head. Instead of letting him have some down time, you see this as an opportunity to tell him what else you need done around the house. After all, it's not like you are going out tonight. Do you see how quickly we can make our needs bigger than our spouse's needs? This is where the platinum rule comes into effect. If he needs some down time rather than going to dinner, put his needs first in this instance. Treat him the way he wants to be treated.

Avoid Distractions When Serving

There are many distractions that take your attention away from your number one priority–your family. If you spend more time away from your family than you do with your family you may need to reevaluate your priorities. You are required to serve your wife like Christ served the church. As a wife you want to honor and respect your husband like that relationship with Christ and the church. Are you serving your spouse to the best of your capabilities? Are you serving willingly? God so loved the world that He gave his only begotten son. God loved us enough that He sent his son to serve us in the form of our own image. Christ gave of himself willingly and unselfishly. He prayed and served even when others tried to distract Him from his ministry and do Him harm. Imagine where we would be if Christ had been distracted by all the things that happened on his journey. It's a scary thought!

Don't let a storm steer you away from your blessing. When a ship sets sail the captain of the ship has a clear course and direction of how they will navigate the ship to each port of call. He must be deliberate with his decisions because his goal is to make sure that his passengers arrive safely at their final destination. However, there are times when the weather won't allow the ship to head in a certain direction. The captain must protect the safety of his passengers at all costs. He must rely on his crew to help him navigate through the storms ahead.

The crew is behind the scenes but each member has an intricate role in ensuring the safety of the passengers. What is equally important is that they remain focused and not allow any distractions to interfere with the task at hand. If the ship is expected to encounter a storm the entire crew must interpret the readings on the equipment and relay the information to the captain. Then the captain will analyze the data and develop a plan to be executed. Once the plan is finalized, the crew must execute it to the letter.

Much like the ship charting its course, a relationship must be prepared to navigate through choppy waters. Like rapper André 3000 said, "You can plan a pretty picnic but you can't predict the weather." You will experience many seasons in your marriage. As a unit, you must work together to ensure the safety of the passengers on board (you and your family). Each player must serve the other utilizing the equipment provided (God's Word) to interpret the data that is in front of them. They must take time to share and analyze the data, then create a strategy to help them get through the tough times, and execute it. It is critical that each of them not let any distractions interfere with their goal of a healthy, lasting relationship. Just like the ship headed into the eye of the storm, one wrong move could be a monumental catastrophe. There's absolutely too much at stake for each of them to allow any distractions to take them off course.

The Ritz–Carlton Effect

The Ritz–Carlton has been a five–star hotel for over a century. The Ritz' success is tied to its core values. Because the Ritz' employees internalize these core values, the customer experiences those values during their stay. These values have helped the hotel establish long lasting relationships with their guests. Similarly, each of us must have a set of core values that help us establish healthy relationships with one another. Here is a list of the Ritz' core values that it expects each employee to learn and act upon. Do you have a list of your core values?

Ritz Carlton's Service Values

1. I build strong relationships and create Ritz–Carlton guests for life.

2. I am always responsive to the expressed and unexpressed wishes and needs of our guests.

3. I am empowered to create unique, memorable and personal experiences for our guests.

4. I understand my role in achieving the key success factors, embracing community and creating the Ritz Carlton image.

5. I continuously seek opportunities to innovate and improve The Ritz–Carlton experience.

6. I own and immediately resolve guest problems.

7. I create a work environment of teamwork and lateral service so that the needs of our guests and each other are met.

8. I have the opportunity to continuously learn and grow.

9. I am involved in the planning of the work that affects me.

10. I am proud of my professional appearance, language and behavior.

11. I protect the privacy and security of our guests, my fellow employees and the company's confidential information and assets.

12. I am responsible for uncompromising levels of cleanliness and creating a safe and accident–free environment.

The Ritz's values are all about building long, lasting relationships with their guests. If you don't have any core values to help you build long, lasting relationships, get some. The worst thing to do is start a relationship with no values. Just like a ship without a sail, a relationship between two people who do not have values is headed nowhere. Begin by internalizing the values that you would like to see in your mate. Discuss your value system with your partner and learn theirs. This will lay the foundation for a healthy, lasting relationship. Now let's see how we can apply a few of the Ritz' core values to our relationships.

- **Ritz employees make every attempt to make the guest's stay a positive and memorable experience.** Show your spouse that the little things matter. Make a daily effort to show your spouse that you want to serve them each day in a memorable way.

- **Ritz employees address problems and resolve them immediately.** Don't allow problems to fester within your relationship. Address minor concerns before they become big problems.

- **Each Ritz employee is a team player.** Be engaged at home. Let your spouse and children see and feel your support.

- **Ritz employees respect one another.** Honor and respect each other within your marriage. Never dismiss an opinion or concern of your spouse. If it matters to him or her it should matter to you.

- **The Ritz encourages the growth of its employees.** Support and encourage your partner's growth so that the two of you will grow together.

- **The Ritz employees are involved in the planning.** Put a plan together for you and your partner. Communicate with your partner about your plan. It is important to keep them engaged.

- **Ritz employees protect the privacy of their guests.** Respect the privacy of your spouse and children. Don't complain to others about your spouse. Not everyone can keep a secret.

 # Real Talk with Chris

As a Marine, I understood service but I did not understand how to serve in my relationship. I thought I could handle things myself, I soon learned I could not. Although I thought I was serving my family (e.g. cooking, cleaning and providing) I was really serving and catering to my own needs more than theirs. I thought I was doing just what the doctor ordered. As it would turn out, I had the order all wrong.

I didn't know the importance of paying attention to the small things— the check–ins or serving with a smile. Selflessness mattered more than I imagined. My former spouse and I needed an intervention *on how to serve one another. I was optimistic that together we could find solutions through the church, mentors and our circle of friends. We tried to surround ourselves with people who believed in their marriage vows and subscribed to the power of prayer.*

Unfortunately, that intervention didn't come soon enough before Murphy's Law kicked in. I soon began to focus more on what she wasn't doing for me than what she was doing overall. I started keeping score and comparing what I was doing for her to what she was doing (or was not doing) for me. Our tanks began to run low and were soon on empty.

Remember this: what you go through to serve others is more for your spiritual development than it is for theirs. What if God is trying to build your character by removing the chinks in your armor? Many times you don't understand why you are going through a storm until it is over. God's plan for us is bigger than our own.

"And we know that in all things God works for the good of those who love him, who have been called according to his purpose" (Romans 8:28)

🎴 **Can We Talk?** 🎴

Questions for you and your partner

The following questions will allow you to assess where you are on your journey to oneness with your spouse and God.

1. When you think of service what comes to mind?

   _____

   _____

   _____

2. How do you show service to your partner?

   _____

   _____

   _____

3. What does service look like to you? What are some of the ways that your partner can serve you?

   _____

   _____

   _____

4. What are some of the ways that you can serve your partner when you don't feel like serving?

   _____

   _____

   _____

5. In what ways can you serve your partner on a daily basis implementing the 5:1 rule?

    _____

    _____

    _____

6. What do you want your partner to start doing, stop doing, and/or continue doing?

Notes:

_____

_____

_____

_____

_____

5

The 5 C's of a Healthy and Lasting Relationship

After experiencing a failed marriage, I developed the 5 C's. I believe these principles are at the core of every healthy relationship. Each of these C's is vitally important to long–term growth. Any couple that fully embraces and understands the importance of each has a greater opportunity to achieve a healthy and lasting relationship.

1 **Christ** – The Bible teaches us that Christ is the foundation of our relationship with our Father in heaven. "I am the way and the truth and the life. No one comes to the Father except through me. If you really know me, you will know my Father as well. From now on, you do know him and have seen him." (John 14:6–7). Similarly, He is the foundation of our relationships with one another.

In the construction industry, one of the most important jobs starts with laying the foundation. The foundation has to be poured and given the proper time to settle before the structure can be built upon it. If the foundation isn't given enough time to settle then the structure will not be adequately supported. If the structure is built on top of a cracked foundation it will cause serious problems down the road.

Just like a house, it is important that your relationship be built on the right foundation. Next, you want to make sure that the house is made of materials that will last. A house built with brick is much stronger than the house built with straw. Much like that of a solid house, if you build your relationship with Christ as the foundation it has the basis to last over the test of time.

It is critical that you keep God at the center of your relationship. If you begin the relationship by leading with the desires of your flesh then you will fall by your flesh. This means that if you begin fueling your relationship with sex, drugs or other damaging and distracting behaviors, these same things can cause you to lose your relationship later. It becomes nearly impossible to satisfy the desires of your flesh. It's like something eating you from the inside out. By giving into your desires, you therefore jeopardize whatever stability your relationship had at the outset. Typically, when a foundation of a house or building is built with cracks and the cracks are not repaired, the integrity of the structure is at risk. Unrepaired cracks often spread over time and cause foundation failure. Cracks, no matter how small, must be immediately addressed to prevent sagging walls and the possibility of foundation failure.

Beloved, just like the foundation of a home or building, all cracks in your relationship with God must be addressed. To prevent foundation failure from happening in your relationship with your spouse, your relationship with God must be solid. He must be the one you go to when things go awry in your life. You must rely on His Word for guidance and answers when you don't know what to do. God gives you the ability to see things His way when you apply the teachings of His Word. When

your relationship is planted in the proper soil and nurtured by Christ it can grow to unlimited potential.

When there are cracks within the foundation of your relationship, it might be time to bring in an expert to assess the situation and advise you on how to prevent the cracks from spreading. Many of us do not like the idea of consulting help but the Bible teaches us that pride goes before destruction. In many instances you've got to swallow your pride, to have a healthy, lasting relationship. The situation is much bigger than YOU. Now is not the time to let your ego prevent you from getting the help and support that you need to keep your relationship moving in the right direction. "How much better to get wisdom than gold... Whoever gives heed to instruction prospers and blessed is the one who trusts in the Lord" (Proverbs 16:20).

If your relationship has a crack in the foundation you can't take it for granted. Don't assume that everything will fix itself. Even the smallest cracks can cause problems over time. It can't hurt to seek professional help. It is strongly recommended that you and your partner discuss your comfort level with counseling. It's never too soon to have a mediator or a Christian advisor help you grow and nurture your marriage.

Why do you call me, 'Lord, Lord,' and do not do what I say? As for everyone who comes to me and hears my words and puts them into practice, I will show you what they are like. They are like a man building a house, who dug down deep and laid the foundation on rock. When a flood came, the torrent struck that house but could not shake it, because it was well built. But the one who hears my words and does not put them into practice is like a man who built a house on the ground without a foundation. The moment the torrent struck that house, it collapsed and its destruction was complete.

Luke 6:46–49

There's nothing wrong with working with a coach. One of the most sought after life coaches in the world is Anthony "Tony" Robbins. Over the past 30 years he has trained, coached and helped propel the careers of 3 past presidents, a litany of athletes, and thousands of business leaders nationally and internationally. His coaching techniques and training have helped millions of people to overcome their fears, challenges and obstacles. Through Tony's coaching, many have reached new levels personally and professionally. Seeking a coach or a counselor to help strengthen your relationship can yield manifold results. God is no respecter of persons. What He has in store for you is for you, but you have to be willing to let Him in. God knows that you can't do it all on your own. Find a support system that provides advice and counsel using sound biblical principles and doctrine. *(Sidebar: There is a difference between a coach and a counselor. Coaching is looking into the future. Counseling is looking more at the past.)*

If you are a believer of God's word, it is important that any advice that you get lines up with biblical doctrine and teachings of God's inspired word. "All Scripture is God–breathed and is useful for teaching, rebuking, correcting and training in righteousness, so that the servant of God may be thoroughly equipped for every good work" (2 Timothy 3:16–17). One of the main things that Christ requires us to do is to constantly seek Him for knowledge, wisdom and understanding for He is the foundation of your relationship.

2 **Communication** – Most relationships fail for lack of communication. Communication is not just what you say, but how you say it. It's not just what you do, but how you do it. Thus, communication is both verbal and non–verbal. Men tend to communicate in their actions or lack of actions and women tend to communicate with their words or abundance of words. Ladies, you've got to give him time to digest what you just said before making your next point. Men need a moment to process things. Fellas, women need more details in your communication with them. They want you to be more selective with your words.

Having good communication skills is essential to the success of any relationship. Good communicators listen intensely before speaking. They process what they've heard before responding. "My dear brothers and sisters, take note of this: Everyone should be quick to listen, slow to speak and slow to become angry, because human anger does not produce the righteousness that God desires" (James 1:19–20).

Part of being a good communicator and having a strong relationship requires your willingness to be transparent and vulnerable as you communicate. As a Christian, the other part of a strong relationship requires constant communication with God to allow Him into your heart to make you more like Him. Without this, we would never be anything close to what God wants us to be. "For my thoughts are not your thoughts, neither are your ways my ways," declares the Lord. "As the heavens are higher than the earth, so are my ways higher than your ways and my thoughts than your thoughts" (Isaiah 55:8–9).

It's never too late to start working on your communication skills. You have to begin somewhere. Take a course or find a married couple who you can spend time with and observe their interactions. Some of us are better communicators than others. However, it is a skill that we all can learn. Once you have learned effective communication, it requires practice to sharpen the skill. Focus on your ability to receive feedback, process it and then act on it.

In a relationship each person wants to feel valued and appreciated. Unfortunately, we don't always show it and say it in a way that our spouses will receive and reciprocate. Sometimes when we speak, we don't always consider how our message will be received. When we respond we don't always think about how the other person will interpret our words or actions. This is all part of communication. When communicating with your spouse, you want to listen to understand and speak to be understood. The onus is on you to effectively communicate your message.

To effectively communicate with your spouse and improve your results you must put aside your selfish tendencies. Remember, you are two different individuals. Both of you think and process things differently. It takes openness and honesty, along with time and a constant commitment to improve the communication in your relationship. At the end of the day, you both want the same thing. Don't make it about who is right and who is wrong. In a relationship you can be right, but be so wrong. Everything doesn't have to be a debate. Learn to live, love and laugh together. Don't take every disagreement as a direct attack on your character.

The Marines have always been known as the first line of defense. They lead the way for the rest of the Armed Services to follow. For them to carry out their mission, they must have instructions. This entails a detailed report from the commanders in charge. Each Marine knows that the stakes are high and that the mission is critical. In a combat situation nothing can be implied. Each Marine must understand their role. Each company and squad must be exactly where they need to be, when they need to be there. They know that they must protect the mission and their fellow Marine.

Your relationship is the same. You must focus on you and your partner's life mission, while protecting the sanctity of your vows. Your partner must know that you've got their back at all times, protecting your marriage from any outside attacks. Your relationship also requires effective and detailed communication. It requires that you are paying attention to your partner and concerned about their well being. Your relationship's success depends on it. The difference between the Marine in combat and the couple in their relationship is the type of battle being fought.

Before entering into a combat hotspot, Marines are given a situation report from their Commanding Officer also known as the "CO." The CO gives them a report detailing who, what, when, where and why. He provides them with enough intelligence to keep them from known enemy hot spots. Similarly, in your marriage, you must get your instructions from the Commander in Chief (God). He will communicate with you and give you instructions through His Word on how to succeed on the battlefield of life. God will order your steps, but your marriage must be your top priority. Every decision that you make on the field must come from God. He is the Alpha and Omega.

Learn how your spouse communicates. Ladies, a man goes into shut down mode when the only way that he knows how to communicate isn't working. He needs to hear the words, "I believe in us." Men, you must understand that a woman will typically try being more expressive through questions, gestures, and hints when she is trying to communicate. A woman will broach the subject seeking answers and solutions before she goes into shut down mode. For many men, this is considered a woman's way of nagging him, when she's only looking for a resolution. She might respond this way simply because you haven't put enough details into your answers.

Tools for Improving Your Communication

Here are some of the tools that I learned along my journey. I highly recommend that you add these into your daily communication routines.

- **Check-ins**–One of the tools to help you grow and improve your communication is called a check-in. The two of you should agree when you want to have check-ins. They could happen daily, weekly or monthly. The purpose of the check-in is to strengthen the communication in the relationship by discussing your partner's mental, emotional and physical well-being. Check-ins can also be about finances, family, health, etc. In sum, you all are taking time to make sure your marriage and your family is headed in a direction that is desirable to you both.

- **Question of the Day**–This is another tool to help you improve your communication and deepen intimacy with your spouse. Ask your partner one question for the day and each of you share your response with one another. In the book, *"Love Talks for Couples."* Dr. Gary Chapman and Ramon Presson help provide couples with questions as conversation starters that they can use to help build and deepen intimacy. Ask a question and allow your partner to be open with their response and not feel intimidated by your actions or gestures. This is a moment where you and your partner are working on being transparent without judging the other. At the end of the day you don't own a heaven or hell to put your spouse in. You are each on the same team. Don't attack each other. Friendly fire causes casualties. This isn't a time for you to criticize or condemn. This is a time for you to affirm and forgive.

- **Games**–Choose games that require you to interact and have fun. Don't let your competitive nature defeat the purpose of playing games together. Winning is not everything. This is a bonding exercise so make the best of it and enjoy.

- **Spiritual enrichment**–Attend Sunday worship service and weekly bible study together. After service, set aside time to discuss the message and what you learned. Remember to respect each other's opinions and views.

- **Workshops/seminars**–Attend workshops together that will help you develop as a couple.

- **Team building exercise**–Try a team building exercise that will allow you to work together while depending on one another to complete the task.

- **Books**–Choose a book or a periodical that you both would read and discuss your views and opinion.

- **Dancing**–Dancing allows you to build trust and encourages a healthy dialogue of fun and communication. Try ballroom, salsa, stepping or hand dancing.

3 **Commitment** – God showed His love and commitment to us by sending His son, Jesus Christ to die for our sins (John 3:16–17). God wants commitment from you and me. He wants us to commit to living for Him and allowing Him to accomplish His plans for our lives in our lives. "Therefore, I urge you, brothers and sisters, in view of God's mercy, to offer your bodies as a living sacrifice, holy and pleasing to God—this is your true and proper worship. Do not conform to the pattern of this world, but be transformed by the renewing of your mind. Then you will be able to test and approve what God's will is — his good, pleasing and perfect will" (Romans 12:1–2).

Everything that you do has some level of commitment involved. Commitment is all about being where you're supposed to be, or doing the things that you are supposed to do when you need to do them. Life is a series of commitments from child hood to adult hood. Children first experience commitment from their parents. They watch their parents go to work each day and pay the bills to put a roof over their head and clothes on their back. Now that's commitment.

Some of you may have been introduced to commitment through youth sports. From the time you were first enrolled in peewee league you were told where to be and when to be there. Commitment is more than just showing up. Commitment is about being engaged and dedicated to giving your best each and every time you step on to the field. Commitment starts with your mindset and willingness to take action. When you make a commitment to participate in team sports you are essentially making a commitment to your teammates. These teammates are relying on you to show up, deliver on your promise and be consistent.

Love and Football

Every summer, 32 NFL teams across the country get together and hold training camp. Training camp is an opportunity for new players and veteran players to showcase their talents and prove to the trainers, coaches and owners that they have what it takes to be selected for the squad. Each team will start their training camp with anywhere from 100 players at the beginning of camp, but by September 1 they must have made their final selections narrowing the roster down to 53 players total. Whether you are a walk–on, rookie, or returning veteran, you must be committed to proving your skills on and off the field.

Each player has to prove that they deserve to be there by demonstrating their dedication, commitment, skill level, and competitive advantage.

Every performance is stack ranked against the rest of the field. This is an opportunity for the players to demonstrate to the coaches that they are the best candidate for the job. For the players it is a brutal test of will power, fortitude and stamina from sun up to sun down. This is where the rubber meets the road and the cream rises to the top. Each position is earned and not given. For the players, commitment involves more than just words; it's about focus and action.

Having a healthy and lasting relationship requires the same level of commitment, focus, determination and sacrifice. Your commitment is measured by what you say, what you do and how you respond on and off the field. You must be willing to show your commitment to God by living according to His principles for your life.

Abraham and Sarah show us the meaning of commitment. Sarah was so committed to Abraham she was willing to follow him anywhere he went. Abraham stayed committed to growing old with his Sarah and seeing God's promise fulfilled in their lives. Through their faith, God blessed them with a miracle birth with their son Isaac. "Now the Lord was gracious to Sarah as he had said, and the Lord did for Sarah what he had promised. Sarah became pregnant and bore a son to Abraham in his old age, at the very time God had promised him. Abraham gave the name Isaac to the son Sarah bore him" (Genesis 21:1–3).

To be committed, you must demonstrate your willingness to put the needs of your partner first. Just like the football team relying on their defensive line, your partner is relying on you. What you do or don't do matters in your relationship. Failing to commit can lead to serious consequences. It can lead to neglect, disappointment, division, disconnect, strife, anger and other issues. Remember, your commitment is shown through your actions. Now that you have committed to the position, let your actions show that you can walk the walk and talk the talk.

Not All Men Are
Afraid to Commit

Ladies, not all men are afraid of commitment some are just not mature enough. If a man is still playing the field he will definitely not want to be in a committed relationship. Commitment to a player is like kryptonite to Superman. He avoids monogamous relationships at all costs. But for most men, the biggest fear is committing to the wrong woman. The ratio of men to women is typically in favor of men. There are a number of men that feel they have a larger pool of women from which to select a mate. When a man still has a lot of play in him, he'll become overwhelmed by the selection of women that are available for him to choose from. This typically leads to indecision on his part and a fear of commitment.

More often than not, the man with a lot of play in his system doesn't know what he really wants for himself, much less what he's looking for in a woman. He will tell women that he is dating and not ready for commitment, but some women try to convince him that he is. Then they get frustrated over him not wanting to be what he said he didn't want to be in the first place–committed. Not committing gives him the opportunity to experience everything that he likes from multiple woman without committing to any one of them. Pretty soon, he is in a position of control and has selected his "starting lineup."

In his lineup, he has a woman who tells him the things that he likes to hear. She is always boosting his ego. Then he has the woman who has the look that he truly desires, but he won't commit to her because she's emotionally and mentally unstable. (Remember, men are 90% visual.) Then he has the woman with the business mindset, but he questions whether or not, she can handle her role. She's the type that is used to giving orders. He is the most leery of this woman.

Ladies, the real reason he won't tell you the deal, is because he's showing you the deal. You're the option, not the main event. Pay attention to his actions, his body language and his words. If they don't line up, ask him for clarity so that you can have understanding. This is where it is important for you to understand your significance in God's kingdom and know your worth. Don't trade yourself as a penny stock when you should be trading on the NASDAQ. A man will commit when he's ready, but giving him an ultimatum won't work. That will only push him away. This is why it is important to have your own standards. No need to waste your time. He's either going to be all in or he's not. If he says, "I'm going to commit." Does he really mean it? Or is he just going through the motions to pacify you? Does he feel pressured? Or does he see you as marriage material?

When it comes to learning how commitment should look in a relationship effective communication is required. It is critical that you discuss what commitment looks like for you. This is the benefit of implementing the weekly or monthly check–ins. You could be expecting one thing from your partner and they feel like their actions already demonstrate commitment. Don't let your own insecurities destroy your relationship. If something happened to you in a previous relationship, then your partner needs to know. However, if this issue or concern has not been properly addressed it may be time to seek professional help. Brushing the problem under the rug won't solve anything.

Women Want Commitment

Every woman desires to be the one and only queen of her castle. All women want to feel respected and appreciated by their partner. Ladies, stop settling for half of a man. Wait on God and He will send you all of the man that you need in His time. A great majority of women today want to be connected to a man who values her worth and is willing to be in an exclusive, monogamous and committed relationship with her. Some feel as though there a shortage of good men? Others would argue that there are not. Could this be the reason that is making it tougher for a good woman to find a man? Should a woman seek the man? The Bible says, when a man finds a wife he finds a good thing. "He who finds a wife finds what is good and receives favor from the LORD" (Proverbs 18:22).

Most men believe that women want to be in a monogamous relationship filled with romance, love and promise. Because of this most single men feel that a single woman wants to lock him down, especially if he is a man that shows promise, has a purpose and is giving his all to live up to his potential. Men tend to believe that being in a committed relationship comes more naturally for a woman than it does for a man. Is that true? Some women are more in touch with their emotions and feelings than men and want to express their love to one man. Then there are other women who have a phobia of being alone and feel that they need to be in a committed relationship with someone all the time.

At the end of the day a woman seeks to be in a committed relationship for many reasons. She just needs to be sure to read the prospectus on the man she is interested in before she starts investing time, energy and resources into the relationship. A woman should always make sure that she will see a return of investment before she gets involved with any man. If he has clearly stated that he is not interested in having a committed, monogamous relationship and you are, then it's clear that you should not waste your time. Ladies, in this situation you must act as if you are the CEO. Some relationships that you have deserve a PINK SLIP. Don't trip because you have already invested time into being with him. If he has not married you yet, he probably will not. Be faithful and wait on GOD. He knows your heart and your desires. He will answer your prayers and fulfill your needs.

4 **Compromise** – To have a strong relationship, it is critical that both parties understand the importance of compromise. For some it is easier to commit than it is to compromise. Just know that compromise is not bad. It should not be viewed as giving in. In a relationship, compromise means finding a common ground between two opposing views on a particular topic. For example, you and your wife are discussing the before and aftercare provisions for the kids. You are in support of putting the kids in the before and aftercare program, to you it appears as the logical thing to do since you have a demanding position with a very inflexible schedule. Unfortunately, your wife is not in agreement with the aftercare program and wants to come up with a different solution.

Three out of five days a week she is willing to pick the kids up by 3:00 p.m. but she is unable to get them on Tuesdays and Fridays. On the other hand, your work day doesn't end until 5:00 p.m. and your commute is an hour across town. In your opinion, since neither of you have any immediate family resources in the area the logical solution would appear to be the aftercare program. However, your wife is thinking about it from a budgetary perspective and somehow wants you to make the sacrifice and pick them up at 3:00 p.m.

This is just one scenario out of many that could possibly occur in your relationship. It will require teamwork, flexibility and compromise for you to work out tough issues. Both of you are entitled to have an opinion on matters that arise in your household. It's all about finding a resolution that will allow you to move forward as a team. Remember, it's not about YOU. You will have to compromise if you want your relationship to work.

Maybe in the aforementioned scenario you alternate months that your children go to aftercare. Whatever the resolution, it's not about keeping score. Keep in mind you are trying to become a dynamic team headed towards God's desired outcome for your marriage. I urge you to think before you speak and to pray before you make decisions together. God uses compromise to build your character. I urge you to ask God to humble you so you can hear and obey His voice. I would also implore you not to allow your emotions to interfere with your decision–making skills. Challenge yourself to see it from your partner's perspective and come to a resolution that is amicable for both of you.

5 **C.A.R.E–Compassion,** Appreciate, Respect, Encourage. Many of us have a hard time showing others that we care, especially if we've been hurt or have not had a caring role model. If you want your marriage to thrive, you must learn to show your spouse that you care. Just because you know you care does not mean that they do. I have broken it down into four characteristics so that you can see caring in action.

Compassion – To grow your relationship you'll need a compassionate heart towards your spouse. Being *compassionate* means showing kindness and empathy towards him or her. Suppose your wife went to work for nine hours and came home, prepared dinner and completed homework with the kids. Before long she's back up and doing it all over again. Eventually this routine is going to burn her out.

A compassionate man would step in and relieve her of her routines. Surprise her by giving her a day or week off. Take over the cooking and homework responsibilities. Shortly after dinner when the kids go to bed, run her a nice hot bubble bath and give her a non-sexual deep tissue massage. In this instance you are not just telling her that you appreciate her, but you are showing her. You are showing that you care and have compassion for her.

Appreciate – In a relationship, everyone desires to be appreciated by their partner. Appreciation is so basic, and yet so overlooked. Remember, it's the small things that matter most for men and women. The words, "thank you" go a long way. It is important that you practice the most basic courtesies. If your partner brings you flowers, cooks your dinner, surprises you with a nice gift, the least you can say is,

Now we ask you, brothers and sisters, to acknowledge those who work hard among you, who care for you in the Lord and who admonish you. Hold them in the highest regard in love because of their work. Live in peace with each other. And we urge you, brothers and sisters, warn those who are idle and disruptive, encourage the disheartened, help the weak, be patient with everyone. Make sure that nobody pays back wrong for wrong, but always strive to do what is good for each other and for everyone else.

1 Thessalonians 5:12–15

thank you. Show them that you are appreciative of everything that they do. Men and women often feel unappreciated by their partners. The best thing that a husband and wife can do for one another is say, "thank you" or "I appreciate you."

Respect – Respect is something that we all seek and desire from our partners. But men and women have different perspectives on what makes them feel respected. Some men want women to respect them just because they are men. This can be rooted in their cultural background or upbringing. Then there are men who make an honest living and provide for their families. These men don't need a whole lot of recognition. They just want to be respected for what they bring to the table. Then there are men in a more delicate situation where they have a spouse who is in the limelight or who earns more money than they do. They may not be insecure but they do not want to feel emasculated in anyway because she earns more. (*Side bar: Ladies, never break a man down and make him feel that he is not worthy because of the money that you make, or the position that you hold at work. Don't let money or a title place you outside of God's will inside your home.*)

A woman wants respect too. In modern society, two–income households are very common. In the old days, the roles were very different for women. They were homemakers and didn't necessarily have to work outside of the home. Now, the woman's role has evolved and more responsibility has been placed on her than ever before. Thus, she deserves respect at a minimum.

She might be a stay at home mom. She deals with getting the kids to and from school, attends all the field trips, cooks all the meals, handles all the doctors appointments, just to name a few things. She just wants to be respected for putting the kids and her husband first. Respect in this scenario may look like appreciation, but the bottom line is she does not want her role as a mother and wife to be minimized. She is making huge sacrifices for her family.

She could also be a world–class woman; the one who does it all. She goes to work every day, buys groceries, and cooks meals and more. She too, wants to be respected by her husband. But she also wants a break every once and awhile because she goes hard all the time. Fellas, you have to allow your wife to take vacations or short get-aways without YOU. Compliment her so that she doesn't get burned out so quickly. If you don't, someone else will.

Encourage – Fellas, it's not what you say to a woman that matters most; it's how you say it. Are your words uplifting? Remember toxic words destroy and denigrate. You reap what you sow. "Do not be deceived: God cannot be mocked. A man reaps what he sows. Whoever sows

> *Treat people as if they were what they ought to be and you help them to become what they are capable of being.*
>
> Johann Wolfgang
> von Goethe

to please their flesh, from the flesh will reap destruction; whoever sows to please the Spirit, from the Spirit will reap eternal life" (Galatians 6:7–8). If you give her negativity she will reproduce it and give it back to you two-fold. "The tongue has the power of life and death, and those who love it will eat its fruit" (Proverbs 18:21). By encouraging your partner, you speak life and health into your relationship. Women are reproducers; they take whatever you give them and multiply it. Give her groceries – she'll give you dinner, give her a house – she'll give you a home.

Ladies, men need encouragement from you more than you can imagine. What you have to realize is that men are problem-solvers. If you give him a problem or situation, he'll spend time on finding ways to fix it. Although, he has a tough exterior there's a heart and a pulse on the inside. Your words can crush him in an instant. Feed him with positivity and he will give you the world. The challenge for many relationships is that people often focus more on the negative than the positive.

Imagine having a boss who never encourages you but expects to get more out of your performance. Every day you come to work and put your best foot forward but your boss always brings up what you didn't do right. After awhile, this slowly eats away at your positive performance. Had your supervisor chosen their words carefully and encouraged you, you would have tried harder to improve.

Positive energy produces better results than negative energy. Remember, to encourage your spouse. Don't beat them down with your nagging and complaining. It could always be worse. The man with no shoes stops complaining when he sees the man with no feet. It may be hard to do, but if no one encourages you learn how to encourage yourself (and buy your other half a copy of my book).

 # Real Talk with Chris

*W*hen *I reflect on my former marriage, I can only imagine what it would have been had we both really understood and applied each of these 5 C's. I wrote this book with the purpose of helping someone else have a healthy or healthier relationship with their partner. Maybe you are just about to begin your journey or already on your journey. I strongly believe that if the two of you fully understand and apply each of the 5 C's daily, your future will look much brighter.*

I think that most relationships start off in euphoria for the first 12–24 months. This is when it appears as though your partner can do nothing wrong. My relationship was no different. Things appeared one way in the beginning but after living together and dealing with different challenges we soon discovered that our 5 C's were missing. We both believed in Christ but our relationship was not rooted in Him.

As I mentioned in chapter 3, prior to marriage, I had not lived a celibate lifestyle or had a monogamous relationship with the Creator. I focused too much on my desire for sex, rather than my need for emotional and spiritual growth. Ultimately, there was a consequence for my negligence. We both had clouded judgment. We made decisions based on our feelings rather than on God's Word. Yes, we were both saved and had accepted Christ as our Savior but we struggled with Him as our Lord.

We were no different than most "Christians" who went to church and prayed on occasion, but the evidence of our faith was not in the decisions we made. Our foundation was built on shaky ground. The foundation of every relationship is critical. If the foundation is built on the lust of your flesh and not the love of Christ – repent and ask God for a new start.

Can We Talk?

Questions for you and your partner

The following questions will allow you to assess where you are on your journey to oneness with your spouse and God.

1. What are the 3 most important priorities in your marriage or relationship? Why?

   _____

   _____

   _____

2. What is it that you are praying and seeking God for in your relationship?

   _____

   _____

   _____

3. What does commitment mean to you?

   _____

   _____

   _____

4. How do you express commitment in your relationship?

   _____

   _____

   _____

5. On a scale of 1–5, five being the highest, how would you rate your communication skills?

_____

6. How would your partner describe your communication style?

_____

_____

_____

7. How would you describe your partner's communication style?

_____

_____

_____

8. Complete the sentence: I can improve my communication skills with my partner by...

_____

_____

_____

9. On a scale of 1–5, five being the highest, rate yourself on your willingness to compromise?

_____

10. How do you show your partner that you C.A.R.E. (Compassion, Appreciate, Respect, Encourage) on a daily basis?

_____

_____

_____

Notes:

_____

_____

_____

_____

_____

6

Leave the Boardroom
out of the Bedroom

Ordinarily, when a man meets a woman he knows what category he will put her in from the beginning. A friend, friend with benefits, girlfriend or wife/mother. Let me be the first to tell you that he wants to marry the one who can be the girlfriend, the wife and the mother. Allow me to explain. As the girlfriend, he wants you to lure him in with your sexiness and sensitivity to his needs and wants. As the wife, he wants to know that you are more than just the chick on the side. As the mother, he wants to see the nurturing and caring side of you.

If he likes you, he is pondering next steps and examining the relationship to decide where you really fit in. He's asking himself two major questions: "Am I ready to make this move?" And "is she the one?" He wants to marry the one with whom he feels comfortable being himself. He needs to feel that he can trust you with his love and that with you by his side he can accomplish his goals, dreams and aspirations.

But once he marries you, he is still looking for the girlfriend. He wants to see your sex appeal and everything that comes with it. Remember, men are visual. He is stimulated by seeing your sexiness all day, every day. He wants to walk into the house and see you cooking in the kitchen with a teddy and five-inch stilettos. He still likes what he likes. In the words of Marvin Gaye, he wants "sexual healing." He is aroused by your naked body as you walk around the bedroom and to the shower strutting in your birthday suit. He gets aroused when he thinks of the countless ways he can be sexual with you.

In his mind, he imagines exploring every part of your body in every area of the house. (*Side bar: Ladies, if this is grossing you out pause for a moment and think of him having these thoughts about another woman. My goal is not to upset you but I want you to realize how your husband WANTS to feel about you.*) He wants spice and spontaneity more than just once a month. He wants what you were willing to do as the girlfriend (before you were washed and cleansed by the blood of Jesus). Now that you are the wife, he is NOT looking forward to seeing long flannel pants and grandma panties along with the Aunt Jemima scarf wrapped across your head all the time. Most men will make an exception and give you a pass if it's that time of the month, and only then. He wants the lady during the day but he wants the freak to come out at night.

If you think I am being unholy or ungodly, you better read your Bible. "Marriage should be honored by all, and the marriage bed kept pure, for God will judge the adulterer and all the sexually immoral" (Hebrews 13:4). Did you read that? The marriage bed is undefiled. That means as long as the relationship is bound in Holy matrimony, two people can have a booty-smacking, hair pulling good time. (*Side bar: If you are not married and enjoying nature's nectar, you are outside of God's will and exposing yourself to serious danger. Can a man hide fire under his coat and not get burned? NO!*)

He likes what He likes

It's important that you capture his mind in the bedroom. If you don't the devil will. The devil is always busy looking for a house to destroy. He starts with the man because the man is the head. The head represents the covering for the family and if the head is attacked the body will fall. Ladies, men are constantly bombarded with thoughts and images of scantily dressed women throughout the day. All he has to do is step out of his office for lunch and he will pass one or two provocatively dressed ladies advertising their sex appeal seeking to capture a man.

Images are constantly trying to penetrate a man's mind. Statistics show that most affairs begin in the work place. The work place is where a person spends the majority of their day and becomes comfortable with those who are around them. Men need to be connected on the home front to avoid the possibility of an attack in the work place. A man who makes love to his wife several times throughout the week is not as likely to succumb to the visual images that are constantly attacking his mind.

Ladies, your husband doesn't always want to be the pursuer, he too likes to be pursued. Although men are hunters, he doesn't mind being the prey when it comes to sexual healing. Mix it up and try something outside of the norm. If you normally have sex in one or two positions, switch it up. Variety is the spice of life. Also, make sure there is enough room in your schedule for "overtime." He doesn't always want a quickie.

Men go to strip clubs to see what they can't see at home. If you want to keep him excited show him that you have some moves of your own. This isn't the time to show him that you are the tongue talking, fire baptized, sanctified and Holy Ghost–filled woman that you might be. You can be born again, and still drop it like it's hot for your husband. This is the time to give him what he likes, how he likes it, for as long as you are both in agreement.

Remember, sex does not give a man an emotional connection. However, in order for him to have an emotional connection with his wife, sex is a requirement. Why fault him for wanting YOU? It could be someone else.

Part of the way that men express their love is through physical intimacy. Don't make him feel like a pig or a pervert for wanting to get down with his wife. This is one of the ways that God gave us to connect with our spouses.

Women do several things that kill intimacy in the bedroom. Ladies, let me share a few things with you that you don't want to do. Don't bring your problems into the bedroom. Whatever, your challenge was throughout the day handle it before you go to bed at night. This is a major issue for a man. His bedroom is his sanctuary. This is the place where he worships with you. If he feels you always have something else on your mind when the two of you lay down at night, he may feel like you are not interested in having sex with him. This opens the door for temptation to creep up in your marriage.

Don't reject him repeatedly. This can be very traumatic and cut him in the worst way. Your man can handle many things, but the one thing that he doesn't want is to feel like he is less than a man. If you continuously reject him, he will feel like he cannot please you. He wants to know that he is fulfilling your desires in and out of the bedroom. He likes to know that each time the two of you are physically intimate he is providing for your needs too. This makes him feel 8 feet tall.

Don't fake an orgasm. You may have heard the saying "fake it 'til you make it." That does not apply in the bedroom. Your husband wants sexual intimacy to feel natural but he also wants it to feel real. He wants to please you and hit all of your erogenous spots. If you are faking it and he finds out, this can be very damaging to the fabric of the relationship.

Don't lose confidence in yourself. If a woman is not confident, sex will feel like a job that she has to do on a certain day at a certain time. This will make it a mechanical experience for both of you. If you are unsure of yourself, pick up a few books on the art of love making and educate yourself on how the pros get down. Then try some of these things with your partner. You'll discover there is a whole world to explore when it comes to sex. Take your time. Try new things. Don't be shy. But be comfortable. Learn to relax and feel confident with your mate. If you have problems in this area, be honest with him or her so that they can help boost your sexual self-esteem.

Ladies, in a man's eyes he considers himself to be very simple; he likes what he likes in the bedroom. It's not rocket science. If you give him what he likes in the bedroom and explore some of the things in his imagination, he will give you the world.

She Wants What She Wants

What is romance? Romance is how one expresses their attraction or their feeling towards another person.

Women don't just want sex and they don't just want to be looked at as sex toys. However, when it comes to her husband, she wants to feel as though she is still the sexiest women in the world. She wants her husband to court her. She needs to feel a continuous connection to her spouse. Women want your actions and your words to show them just how much they are appreciated. Women need romance and intimacy. They need gentleness, passion and foreplay. And sometimes she may just want to cuddle and talk.

For a woman to get the most out of physical intimacy, they must have an emotional connection. This connection can happen in a number of different ways. She may feel emotionally connected when you speak her love language. She may feel emotionally connected to you by your honesty. She may feel emotionally connected to you because she trusts you. Another way of emotionally connecting with you could come from how secure she feels when she's with you; she feels like she can let her guard down. Again, she wants what she wants.

For a woman, love making starts with her mind and emotions. Once you have captured those two things, she will anticipate becoming physically intimate with you. Women are wired differently. They are nurturers and reproducers. For a woman, physical intimacy has to have meaning and purpose. It's more than going through the motions. She is giving up and releasing an important part of herself. Therefore, she wants and needs to feel loved by her husband.

Women are wired for romance. Romance allows her to feel *desired*. When she receives romance, it is natural for her to reciprocate what you want and need. Typically, she will give back to you two–fold above and beyond what she receives. Make no mistake about it though, she still wants you to explore every area of her body and show patience while doing it. She wants you to know her likes and dislikes as well as you know the lyrics to your favorite song.

For a woman, romance doesn't vanish when you say, "I do." It's a lifelong requirement. Romance doesn't mean you say "hi" in the morning and then expect to jump her bones at night. No! There's more to it than that. Remember, women are wired differently. Romance starts in the morning when she wakes up. Start her off by serving her breakfast at the kitchen table with a vase of flowers and a special card that tells her how beautiful she is and how much you appreciate her. Before she leaves for work, have a sticky note lying across the steering wheel of her car that says, "You mean the world to me, I love you." Send her text messages with little kisses or hearts throughout the day. Call her up on the job just to say, "I love you."

It's important to know that women need a reason to make love. Therefore it takes her more time to get into the mood. Be patient with her. Be gentle with her. Create the atmosphere for her by stimulating her mind with great conversation. This will allow her to relax and start to shift the focus from work to you. Treat her like the finest vintage automobile. Her engine takes time to warm up. All of her pistons don't just fire right away. The more attention you give her, the more she will feel loved, appreciated and will give back to you. She still wants what she wants.

He Wants to Fulfill Your Needs so Teach Him

I already mentioned that you should never fake the orgasm. If you do, he will never know what it's like to fully please you and take you there. You're selling him short. He will feel cheated. Your actions from this point out, dictate the course of the relationship. Ladies it's a hit or miss subject, but it has to be ever so carefully shared. If what he is doing is not working for you, teach him how.

He wants to fulfill all of your needs. Teach him how to make love to your mind and your body. Be patient with him and you show him how to explore every area of your body. It is important that you have a discussion about this area of your relationship in the very beginning. Remember, men have egos and think that they are always on their "A–game" in the bedroom. Take time to explore your options together and help him learn how to please you. If he is too quick to the finish line, invest in a topical solution that will decrease his sensitivity.

If you like lotions, potions and creams, share them with him. Show him how to apply them. If you like foreplay, try playing games that add fun and excitement for both of you. There are a number of games available that you can play that will allow you to take turns and enjoy the pleasures that come with it. It means a lot to a man to hear and see your body respond to certain kisses, touches and movements. When he does it right, give him instant feedback. This will allow him to be more aggressive and in tune to the things that you need. As he learns your body, he will develop a certain level of confidence and exude the swagger that will drive his inner man. He is ready and willing to conquer deeper levels of intimacy with you. He yearns for the opportunity to take you to higher sexual peaks.

If you want to try toys, talk to him about his willingness to venture down that road. Be careful. Some men are not confident in this area as it could expose his internal insecurities. Not all men are willing to allow toys into the bedroom. He may take issue that the toy can please you in a way that he cannot. This could lead to mental challenges or could emasculate him. If he is secure, take him on a field trip to your local exotic store. Have fun with it. As long as you both are in agreement be open and make the best of it.

Stop Using Sex as a Bargaining Chip

The Bible teaches us that within marriage, we should acquiesce to our spouse's needs for physical intimacy. If you are withholding sex, it should be mutually agreeable for a specific reason and should be short-term.

Ladies, don't use sexual intimacy as a bargaining chip. Sex should not be used as a reward for good behavior or to manipulate him to do the things you want done around the house. If you are not getting through to him with your communication don't use sex as a get back. There are other methods. He will grow weary of hearing the words, "I'm tired."

Men, you have to understand that your woman connects with the simplest things. She wants to know that she is on your heart and mind throughout the day. Show her that she is more than just an act from your favorite pornographic movie. Show her that she is appreciated. Don't just touch her when it's time for some sexual intimacy. Hold her hand, kiss her and hug her in public and in front of the kids. Be an example of how a man should show tenderness and love towards his wife. Also, if you notice that she is busy around the house, lighten her load. She wants to feel connected to you throughout the day before she can connect with you between the

The husband should fulfill his marital duty to his wife, and likewise the wife to her husband. The wife does not have authority over her own body but yields it to her husband. In the same way, the husband does not have authority over his own body but yields it to his wife.

1 Corinthians 7:3-4

sheets. This way, she may actually want to initiate intimacy with you. Imagine her bragging to her girlfriends about you like Song of Solomon 5:10-16 (see right).

You might be saying, "Yeah right, Chris. My wife would never say anything like this." Try connecting with her for one week without expecting anything and watch her inner–sex goddess come out. Her words may not be as eloquent as those from the Song of Solomon, but she will tell somebody about how good her man is! Trust me.

The Body is the Temple – Protect It

As we age the body changes. It is important to be healthy and watch what you eat. There are plenty of studies that link sexual desire to healthy living. Eating the right foods along with proper exercise can dramatically add years to your life. Losing weight stimulates blood flow, builds confidence, improves stamina and enhances performance in the bedroom.

Ladies, he understands that you are the wife and the mother. However, he still remembers how you looked in the beginning. A man likes to see you fit and healthy. He knows that if he mentions your weight at all, he could be relegated to prisoner status in his own home (no home–cooked

My beloved is all radiant and ruddy, distinguished among ten thousand. His head is the finest gold; his locks are wavy, black as a raven. His eyes are like doves beside springs of water, bathed in milk, fitly set. His cheeks are like beds of spices yielding fragrance. His lips are lilies, distilling liquid myrrh. His arms are rounded gold, set with jewels. His body is ivory work, encrusted with sapphires. His legs are alabaster columns, set upon bases of gold. His appearance is like Lebanon, choice as the cedars. His speech is most sweet, and he is altogether desirable. This is my beloved and this is my friend, O daughters of Jerusalem.

Song of Solomon 5:10–16

> Do you not know that your bodies are temples of the Holy Spirit, who is in you, whom you have received from God? You are not your own; you were bought at a price. Therefore honor God with your bodies.
>
> 1 Corinthians 6:19–20

meals and no nookie). Most women are sensitive about their weight. Thus, men feel as though they can't be truthful in this department without suffering cruel and unusual punishment.

A secure man does not want to shatter his woman's confidence. But he wants to be honest with you about becoming the best you that you can become. A man with children respects and loves you for having his children, but he hopes that you will still be the eye candy that he had before the babies. He doesn't want you to let yourself go. He still likes what he likes.

A woman puts more focus on what's inside of the engine than outside of the engine. But when it comes to physical enjoyment, she wants him to be healthy enough to meet her needs in and out of the bedroom. Most of the time she will sacrifice what she really wants to please him. She takes great pleasure that he is able to enjoy himself. She knows that there are times that call for a quick lube, and other times that call for a complete tune-up. No matter what the order calls for she needs him to be healthy enough to enjoy it.

To please his wife, he may have to lose a few inches around the midsection. When a man has adopted an unhealthy lifestyle, it can alter his ability to deliver the results in the bedroom. A woman who loves her husband will accept certain changes he may go through with age because she is more apt to focus on the core of who he is, rather than how he looks and how he performs in the bedroom. But don't get it twisted. She still wants to be treated like she is the apple of her man's eye. This is where a man should appreciate a woman who isn't always focused on sex.

This is a great opportunity to put a fitness plan together and spend some quality time burning those inches away. Despite the fact that you both have hectic schedules, it is important to find 2–3 days per week for 30–minutes of fitness. Journal your results as you burn those inches and calories away. This is a great time to encourage each other as you strive to develop a healthier lifestyle and rebuild your temple. Make it fun, be playful and create lasting moments together. Tell each other how good you look and be supportive of each other along the journey.

 Real Talk with Chris

There are many men who want to feel passion with their partner in the bedroom. They want the lady to present in the boardroom, but be willing bring out the alter ego in the bedroom. They want to break away from the standard routine by trying new, creative and adventurous things in the bedroom. I was no different. As I shared in chapter 3, I was obsessed with the visual images and fantasies that I desired to act out. Little did I realize how much of my actions were led by the desires of my flesh rather than love for my wife. We live in a sex driven society that says, "you can have it your way." What I didn't realize was the effect that it had on my ex– wife. Yes, I still liked what I liked but I wasn't willing to give her what she wanted early on in the relationship. I wasn't giving her the romance, conversation and other things that would feed her soul and boost her desire to be intimate with me.

In chapter 3, I posed the question, "What is Love?" Ladies, you have to teach a man how to love you. I did not know how to love myself first so I could not love my wife. I didn't really connect the dots until I sought the assistance of a counselor six years into our marriage. We were at a place where we needed a positive change.

Unfortunately, it was too late. My ex–wife did not attend counseling with me so I went alone. After a couple of sessions, the counselor shared that she could not deal with me until she could deal with us. She needed the other side of the story. I convinced my ex– wife to attend and she went to a couple of sessions but her heart was not in it. She eventually revealed to me that she wanted a divorce.

I share all of this to say, that it is imperative that you address issues before they pop up in the relationship or soon afterwards. When it comes to sex, I learned that for a woman to feel comfortable releasing in the bedroom she has to feel good about herself, secure within herself, secure within the relationship and feel connected to YOU. Otherwise, she will just be going through the motions.

Looking back on it, I think my ex–wife may have brought work or other distractions into the bedroom merely because I didn't connect the dots with her on an emotional level. I needed to focus on the small things that she needed throughout the day (e.g. a call, text, card, e–gram, etc.)

Conversely, a man doesn't need the same thing. But he needs sex. If his sexual appetite and imagination aren't being fulfilled, then this could lead to him seeking it through other means. It did for me. Although I never stepped out of the relationship, I began to consume pornography. I did this in secrecy hoping that my partner would not find out. Sadly, she did. This made an already strained situation more complicated. I learned that it is a woman's desire to please her husband, but she doesn't want to compete with the internet.

 Can We Talk?

Questions for you and your partner

The following questions will allow you to assess where you are on your journey to oneness with yourself and God.

1. Do you have a pattern of bringing work home and into the bedroom?

   ☐ Yes ☐ No

2. How has it affected your intimacy in the bedroom? Why?

   _____

   _____

   _____

3. What are your thoughts, feelings, and expectations about sex?

   _____

   _____

   _____

4. What does romance mean to you? How does it look? How do you respond to it?

   _____

   _____

   _____

5. Complete the following sentences: I feel connected to you when…I like it when you…

   _____

   _____

   _____

6. I am committed to doing more...

_____

_____

_____

7. What behaviors do you need to adjust when it comes to food? How can your spouse support you?

_____

_____

_____

8. How do you feel about fitness?

_____

_____

_____

9. What do you feel is hindering you from achieving your desired goal?

_____

_____

_____

10. What are your health concerns, if any?

_____

_____

_____

Notes:

_____

_____

_____

_____

7

Money

On our journey we have discussed several key ingredients towards having a healthy relationship. Now it's time to discuss money. This is one of the biggest challenges in a relationship. Money is one of the top reasons for divorce. Money is something that we all need, but why does the lack or abundance of it effect our relationships the way it does? I don't know the answer to that but there are ways to avoid major conflicts over money. The keys are communication and planning.

I believe that many people go into a relationship without a blue print for financial success. All too often, the expectations regarding money (e.g. spending, saving, investing) are not clearly defined. You both have an opinion and need to share your thoughts. If you are single and considering marriage you really need to know how this person views money. It is highly critical before going into a marriage relationship that you discuss your expectations, thoughts, feelings and beliefs over how you and your partner handle money.

You may have learned proper money management skills such as creating a budget, balancing a checkbook, setting aside a percentage of your income and then paying your tithes and offerings. Your spouse may have come from a home where one of the parents was a spendthrift and very irresponsible with money. Regardless of your different backgrounds, it is highly advised that you devise a plan. Maybe you are currently married–it's not too late to get a plan. Without a plan you expose yourself to greater risk and unfulfilled expectations. Don't be foolish. You also need to get a clear understanding of your potential partner's debt situation and their plan to resolve it.

Are you discussing the tough questions upfront? What is the short and long range plan to payoff the debt? What happens if one of you loses a job? What's your contingency plan if you have to shut down the business? If you were financially strapped what could you both live without? What is the plan if one of you gets sick and you have to tap into savings? The Bible says that, "my people are destroyed from lack of knowledge" (Hosea 4:6). The question is: are you entering into relationships ill–prepared and setting yourself up for failure?

Learning to Work Together

When you come together in the union of marriage it is no longer *your* money, *your* issues or *your* savings. It is now *"ours."* What happens next? This is where it is vitally important to learn how to work together. You can no longer look at things as "mine." You are not in competition with each other. If you foster a competitive environment around finances you will be setting yourself up for frustration and divisiveness in your union. This only creates animosity, alienation and distrust. Your past money management choices are a place of reference. Don't let previous bad decisions

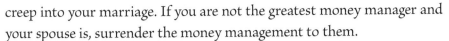

creep into your marriage. If you are not the greatest money manager and your spouse is, surrender the money management to them.

One of the benefits of marriage is partnership. This means you don't have to know everything. Humble yourself and work together. Allowing your partner to teach you about money or handle the finances does not give them a proxy to make decisions without you. Your opinion still matters. Remember, one of the goals within your marriage is to be more Christ–like by glorifying God and modeling the relationship between Christ and the Church. Jesus taught His disciples how to be disciples by modeling the behavior. He was compassionate, loving, kind, patient and giving. You have to model the same behavior while teaching your spouse.

Today, there are many successful marriages that choose to work together by bringing all of their resources together For example, they might deposit their paychecks into one primary joint account. It is from that account that they pay their tithes, mortgage/rent and other household expenses. They use subsidiary joint accounts for things like savings, vacation, emergency and miscellaneous. Every pay cycle after the primary expenses have been covered they give themselves an allowance into their miscellaneous accounts earmarked for their respective pleasures. The miscellaneous account provides them with their own autonomy to spend money on the things that they wish to buy.

The most successful marriages buy into the philosophy of combining resources for the good of the family's long term success. They strive for oneness in all areas of their relationship including their finances. They will typically set a dollar limit for all major purchases. Many couples find that setting limits cuts down on the feeling of anxiety that comes from not knowing what your partner is spending. It also helps remove the fear of not being able to carry your financial load. When all of the resources are combined it is no longer about what you have – it's about what we have. Lastly, it helps improve trust between both parties.

Don't Let Poor Decisions Today Control Tomorrow

Make sound decisions today because they will have an impact on tomorrow. Don't let money control you. Actively manage your money. We reap what we sow. What are you sowing into in your relationship? Are your poor financial choices leading your relationship towards self–destruction? Don't let our materialistic society influence your choices. Whether you are in a good financial position or not, is it really necessary to try to keep up with the Joneses? As long as you and your partner agree on what you purchase it's fine to get what you want but remember that you don't have to spend it just because you have it. Take a look at your motive behind buying certain items.

Here are several questions that you can ask yourself: *Is this within my budget? Why do I need this? Will this purchase create conflict in my relationship? What is the return on investment that this purchase will bring my family?* You have to be in agreement that neither of you will make large purchases without the other. You don't want to make purchases today, that will cause undue stress later on in your relationship and put you in bondage to debt. "The rich rule over the poor, and the borrower is slave to the lender" (Proverbs 22:7).

Don't let spending ruin your marriage. If you don't control it now you will suffer later. Spending is like a drug– it can alter your thinking and the way you make choices. No one goes into the union of marriage thinking that money will be a huge problem. But two people coming from two different backgrounds must consider financial management before marriage. Financial management is a learned behavior. Maybe you received formal training in this area or maybe you have tried the common sense approach. Either way, it is best that both of you create a plan for your financial future together. Start out with a budget and set goals for paying off debts. There are plenty of online resources that can assist you in this area such as www.SuzeOrman.com or www.MichelleSingletary.com.

You Can't Take It with You

Regardless of whether you're a CEO of a Fortune 500 company or grocery store clerk–you can't take money with you. Maybe you are passionate about your work. Don't allow your passion to turn into greed. Greed clouds good judgment. Greed will lead you down a road of unhappiness. It can even affect your health. No matter how driven you are about your business or your profession there's more to life than money.

For business owners, the challenge is managing the business without becoming overwhelmed. They become so consumed with the day–to–day activities of the business that they develop tunnel vision. Soon the business becomes the top priority, instead of God and family. It becomes all about money and more money. If the family is lucky they fall in third place. Soon the kids have to schedule an appointment just to get on your calendar. You kiss them in the morning just before heading off to work and rush home to see them just before they go to bed. Your children won't remember the money, but they will remember the memories that you create. There's more to life than money. And trust me, it won't help you after you've left the earth.

Maybe you're seeking a promotion on your job, but it requires working an 80 hour week. Is it really worth it? Could this cause additional stress within your marriage? There's nothing wrong with seeking opportunities and wanting more out of life, but if it's going to cause turmoil at home, think twice. Being passionate about your goals is honorable. The problem occurs when you prioritize money at the expense of your family. Maybe you're a hard worker who balances family and work but you don't see the fruits of your labor. Don't get discouraged when you've given it your all and you don't see the harvest coming. Stay the course and keep fighting. You are not the only one experiencing a season of drought or difficulty. Don't feel that it's ok to shut down and isolate yourself from your family and loved ones when life happens to you. That's when you need them the most. There will be seasons in your life that will require sacrifice on the part of both you and your spouse. Learn to discuss your expectations and needs before you get in the midst of a difficult season.

Everybody responds differently to the pressures of life, especially when it comes to money. Some experience anxiety, depression or mood swings due to lack of money. Some feel the same way when they have an abundance of it because they never have enough or they are afraid to lose what they have. Don't be so quick to think the grass is greener on the other side. Whether rich or poor, when we are in Christ there is hope. We can follow the example of Paul. Paul teaches the people of Philippi how to live in prosperity and be filled whether hungry or in need. "I know what it is to be in need, and I know what it is to have plenty. I have learned the secret of being content in any and every situation, whether well fed or hungry, whether living in plenty or in want" (Philippians 4:12).

Real Talk with Chris

Neither I nor my ex–wife grew up with silver spoons in our mouths. But we both had different views on how we spent money and what we spent money on. In the beginning of our relationship, I was the one that wanted the nice car and big house. However, I was also extremely credit conscious and responsible with paying every bill before the due date. My ex–wife was the saver. She could squeeze a dollar out of fifteen cents.

It was through our pre–marital counseling and the teachings of our church that we learned the importance of bringing our resources together as a team. We agreed to combine all of our finances into a joint account. However, prior to meeting my ex–wife I had developed an insecurity complex about money that I carried with me into my marriage.

I'll never forget the dinner date that created the complex. I was in my early twenties at the time. I was asked by a young lady who had invited me out on a dinner date. I accepted the invitation to join her. What I didn't know was that she was asking me out, but expecting me to pick up the tab. That was the problem. My perception was that if a person asks you out, then they would pick up the tab. I would soon learn a very hard lesson. Nothing can be assumed.

The moment the bill came I looked at her and she looked at me. I was surprised and shocked when she asked me if I were picking up the tab. I had $16 in my pocket which was enough to cover my meal, without the tip. Sadly, there was even less money in my Navy Federal Credit Union account. This was also prior to the advent of Visa/MasterCard debit cards. I was embarrassed, but that was not the highlight. The highlight was the fact that I sat at the restaurant table while she drove my car to her bank to withdraw the money. After I dropped her off at her home–we never spoke again.

This was a life changing experience for me. Which leads me to ask the ladies the following questions: If you invite the man out on the date, who pays? Does it make him less of a man, just because he "can't" pay for everything? Is it more important that he have money in his pocket, or be a man of character and substance that can treat you right?

This experience left me feeling rejected, confused, and inadequate as it pertained to relationships and money. If I had I stayed within my budget to begin with, learned how to plan and communicate this situation would have never occurred.

This experience was the bag of garbage that I would bring with me into my relationship with my former wife. Every time we went on a date I would ask the question are you paying or am I? She would ultimately ask me to stop. I am certain that it use to irk her nerves. I was still shocked and traumatized from that date at the restaurant.

You can see the subject of money can create challenges in any relationship. Eventually my ex–wife and I would get through these challenges. We linked all of the accounts together. We established basic rules regarding money and expenditures. We set boundaries around major purchases. We were in sink and in stride.

Shortly thereafter, I got the entrepreneurial bug. In 2002, I began my real estate career This was also during the time when the market was just about to go into the biggest real estate boom the country had ever seen. By 2005 I was making more money in one month than I did in a year in any of my former jobs. Things were good. I was laser focused on my goals year after year. Unfortunately, I didn't notice that my spouse and I were really growing apart until it was too late.

I thought life was good since we were in a position to take 2–3 vacations a year and pay our bills on time. I didn't fully understand the damage that was created from my previous failed business ventures. I didn't understand the strain that I put on her. I didn't see that my ambitious nature was taking a toll on her patience. I didn't see that her belief in me was wearing down. I didn't understand how it really made her feel to see a real estate settlement fall apart at the last hour when we were counting on that money for bills or Christmas gifts. I didn't see and understand her concern when the real estate market started to spiral downward and she wanted me to get another job. I didn't know that she was really saying she didn't feel secure. Through this experience I learned that women need security.

I believed in me and my abilities, but I could not control the circumstances of the market. As hard as I wanted to hold on to my dreams, the ship went down faster than I could have imagined. Within the timeframe of 3–years (2007–2010), my real estate business suffered a tremendous loss. Sadly I had not planned any safety nets for my family in the event I lost my primary source of income. I lived based on what my income was rather than on an actual budget. I eventually had to make some tough decisions and cut out two events that I sponsored which meant a lot to me. One of those events was the annual golf tournament that I hosted for a small local non–profit for kids with asthma and the other was my annual clients and friend's holiday party. When I talk of money management, I am speaking from experience. Each of my experiences have taught me that I need to trust in God more than myself.

 Can We Talk?

Questions for you and your partner

The following questions will allow you to assess where you are on your journey to oneness with yourself and God.

1. On the scale of 1–5 (five being excellent), how are you with managing your money?

   _____

2. What are your challenges with money and saving? What things can you do differently?

   _____

   _____

   _____

3. What are your thoughts, feelings, and misconceptions regarding money?

   _____

   _____

   _____

4. Describe how you feel or act when you have a lack or abundance of money? (Depressed, angry, moody, despondent, happy, sad, anxious, guilty, shameful, envious etc.) Describe your actions towards your spouse, family or others?

   _____

   _____

   _____

5. Which partner manages the finances for the household? What are your thoughts regarding what you'd like to start, stop, and continue doing?

_____

_____

_____

6. Have you created a budget? Have you been able to live within the confines of the budget? What's the short–term plan?

_____

_____

_____

7. I think we should...

_____

_____

_____

8. I need to... So that we can...

_____

_____

_____

9. I am out of balance when...

_____

_____

_____

10. Do you seek God when making financial decisions?

_____

Notes:

_____

_____

_____

_____

_____

8

The Man in the Mirror

I n January 1988, Michael Jackson released his hit song, "Man in the Mirror." The famous chorus said, "If you want to make the world a better place, take a look at yourself and make a change."

When I listen to this song, I believe that I can make the world a better place. I have no one to blame for the state of the world, if I am not doing my part to make it better. I have to start with the man in the mirror. Who do you see when you look into the mirror? Or do you avoid looking in the mirror because you don't like what you see?

Most of us men hear competing voices in our minds. This doesn't mean we are schizophrenic, but it means we have fears and doubts looming at us every time we wake up. Civilized society is no different than the jungle when it comes to living a principled life– only the strong will survive. Our culture tells men that success means having a six figure income, a job with a lofty title, living in the best neighborhood, driving the luxury car and holding season tickets for your favorite professional teams.

When a man looks in the mirror he must ask himself one major question: Is the man in me bigger than the God in me today, or is the God in me bigger than the man in me today? He is in a constant battle not to lose his identity and be swallowed by the daily temptations of his flesh. "You, dear children, are from God and have overcome them, because the one who is in you is greater than the one who is in the world" (1 John 4:4).

He wakes up every day with the goal of providing food, shelter and clothing for his family. He knows that, as the man, he must hunt daily for his keep. He knows that it is critical for him to keep a good job and make an honest living to provide for his family's needs. He is all about his hustle as he strives to provide a better lifestyle for his family than the one he had as a child.

If he is a corporate man, he may dream of climbing the ladder to achieve a top executive position. He works tirelessly to prove to himself and others that he is the right man for the job. He competes against his peers and is constantly scrutinized by his supervisors. The decision makers determine if he stays, if he gets a raise and if he is the right fit for their culture based on their perception, opinions and his performance. This is a routine that he must embrace if he is to succeed in corporate America. If he wants to make a career for himself within the company he must learn to play the game. He cannot take the risk of standing out for anything other than exceptional performance.

If he owns a small business or works a blue collar job, he must wake up every day knowing that he will either be the lion or the gazelle and hit the ground running. Every day he is faced with a new challenge. For a man, his work defines his very existence. He constantly tries to one up himself because he feels pressure to be "The Man." Unfortunately, many men become more consumed with their careers and money than with the transformation of their minds to God's purpose for their lives. "Do not conform to the pattern of this world, but be transformed by the renewing of your mind. Then you will be able to test and approve what God's will is—his good, pleasing and perfect will" (Romans 12:2).

No man wants to feel like he is unable to provide for his family. A man is afraid of letting his family down. He wants to be in control. He wants everyone to know that he's got a plan and that everything is going to work out. Rejection can be devastating to his pride and self-esteem. This is where he must be in touch with his inner man and know his self-worth.

Unfortunately, life isn't always predictable and just when he least expects it, he finds himself losing control. He finds himself either in a problem, leaving a problem, or heading towards a problem. The last thing that he wants to do is hit the panic button in front of his family. The man who looks like he has everything going on sees it differently when he looks at the man in the mirror. He's his own worst critic. When he gives his best, he often wonders whether his best was good enough. He requires more out of himself. If he is not careful, he becomes obsessed with the idea of never being good enough.

The Anger in Me Can No Longer Control the Man in Me

The word "father" invokes an immediate reaction from men, which can either be positive or negative. Generations of men have been raised by their mothers, grandmothers and other loved ones. These men stand on the shoulders of many courageous women that were both a mother and a father. However, a woman cannot teach a boy how to be a man. I have met countless men who would have loved the opportunity to create fond and lasting memories with their biological fathers.

When a young man grows up without his father or a father figure, he will often

He will turn the hearts of the parents to their children, and the hearts of the children to their parents; or else I will come and strike the land with total destruction.

Malachi 4:6

look for a role model outside of the home. Some join gangs looking for acceptance and guidance. Street gangs and crews give young men a sense of identity that they crave. They soon learn that this path comes with a guarantee that they will either be incarcerated or buried six feet underground. Our streets have claimed the lives of many great and promising young men.

All too often our boys are part of a never-ending cycle of violence and prison. Some make poor choices because they have no guidance, while others were just at the wrong place at the wrong time. Either way, these young men have to deal with the man in the mirror when it comes to owning up to the decisions they make. For him to move beyond the hurt and disappointment his father's presence or absence may have caused, he must be willing to come to a place of reconciliation.

This comes through growth, maturity and acceptance. He must grow to a place where he can accept the fact that he cannot change the past. Then he must mature to the point where he can forgive his father for everything he did or did not do. The final piece of the puzzle is that a man must realize that he cannot heal all the years of anger, bitterness or sense of abandonment on his own. He must pray and seek God. He must be willing to develop a resolve that the anger in him will no longer control the man in him. No longer can he blame his present problems on the ills of his past. If he is in Christ, he must choose to let go and become the man God created him to be. "If any man be in Christ, he is a new creature: old things are passed away and all things become new" (2 Corinthians 5:17).

There are men who are constantly reminded of their fathers when they look in the mirror. It's as if his father were standing in front of him telling him that he would never amount to anything. These images are engraved in his mind as he strives to provide for his family. The devil knows just how to attack the man in the mirror. He is completely aware of the turbulent or non-existent relationship that the man in the mirror might have had with his father. He will use it in an attempt to destroy his sense of self-worth. It is important to remember that, whether you're biological father was there for you or not, your heavenly Father will supply all your needs. "And my God will meet all your needs according to the riches of his glory in Christ Jesus" (Philippians 4:19).

Don't Let the Shadows of Your Past Hinder the Promises of Your Future

In his book titled, *"Finally Free,"* released in September of 2012, Michael Vick tells his story of failure and redemption. Before his fall, Michael was a highly paid quarterback in the NFL. However, along his journey he made some poor choices, associated with the wrong crowd and encountered some severe setbacks that would forever tarnish his reputation. As he waited to be sentenced to prison for his involvement in an illegal dog fighting ring, Michael was faced with a life changing situation. Some said that he would never play football again. Many wrote him off and dismissed him from the very game that gave him his start.

After serving his sentence, NFL Commissioner Roger Goodell cleared him to play again. Several teams looked at him, but only one team dared to pick him up. That's when it all changed for Michael Vick. The ownership of the Philadelphia Eagles believed in him enough to offer him a one year contract with the 2nd year club option. They gave him a chance to play the game that he loved the most.

Under the leadership of Coach Andy Reid and six–time Pro–Bowl quarterback Donavan McNabb, things turned around for Michael. He let go of his past, the naysayers and the critics and he focused on his game. As a result, in February 2010 the Philadelphia Eagles placed the franchise tag on Michael. He signed a 6–year contract for $100 million. God is not finished with Michael Vick. It was God that gave him the athletic talent that catapulted him to fame and it was God who gave him a second chance.

The moral of the story here is whether it's Michael Vick or you, God is no respecter of persons. Just like Michael, you can declare that you are "finally free." Your past is no indication of what you can become in the future if you keep God first. God can take our past failures and use them for your good. "And we know that in all things God works for the good of those who love him, who have been called according to his purpose" (Romans 8:28).

When I was a child, I talked like a child, I thought like a child, I reasoned like a child. When I became a man, I put the ways of child-hood behind me.

1 Corinthians 13:11

Will the Real Men Please Stand Up?

There comes a time when every man will have to leave behind the childish ways of his past. He will be forced to learn new things and overcome setbacks. The man in the mirror can no longer brag about his past achievements or pout over his past failures. He will have to check his pride at the door. A real man will stop blaming his wife and kids for his problems and instead assess himself as the source of his issues. If the true benchmark of a man is measured by Christ, how do you compare?

So much is at stake if the man in the mirror does not take his rightful place as the head of the household. The real man leads his family according to the principles of biblical teachings. The real man's priorities are faith, family and finances– in that order. Make no mistake about it, there are a lot of men who are holding it down and doing some very positive things. However, if you are a Christian man who is walking by faith, you are held to a higher standard.

Since the beginning of time, we know that real men work to provide for their families. We also know that real men don't beat and abuse their women. Real men don't neglect their children. Real men lead by example. Real men pray. Real men have a compassionate heart towards others. Real men serve God. Real men worship God. Real men cry. Real men love.

The Voices in My Head

Men and women both deal with similar struggles. We can see it from the beginning of time with Adam and Eve. As we read the book of Genesis, we soon see the downfall of a man and woman as they face the same struggles regarding the decisions they make and whose voice they choose to listen to.

There are two voices that we are presented with in every situation. They are the voice of good and the voice of evil. The voice of good is the voice of God. God's voice is usually subtle and provides an inner peace. The other voice is the voice of Satan but it may not sound like him. This voice is crafty and presents itself as the reasonable choice when you are faced with one or more decisions that will impact your life. Ordinarily, this will be the dominant voice inside your head. Satan's goal is to distract you and throw you off course by trying to trick and confuse you.

Just like Adam and Eve, God gives us instructions that are designed to bless and protect us. The question is will we respond to Him the same way that Adam and Eve did? (See Genesis 3:1–13). Or will we follow His voice to avoid sin and the desires of our flesh? Eve clearly heard God's instructions. However, when she was approached by the serpent she heard the enticing lie he told her and chose to listen to the wrong voice.

But I gave them this command: Obey me, and I will be your God and you will be my people. Walk in obedience to all I command you, that it may go well with you. But they did not listen or pay attention; instead, they followed the stubborn inclinations of their evil hearts. They went backward and not forward.

Jeremiah 7:23–24

Your choices have a life and death result. Adam and Eve made a life changing decision that affected us all. Listening to the voice of evil caused the fall of man and introduced sin into this world. Imagine if you could understand why your husband thinks the way he thinks, and why your wife does what she does, you could understand things a little clearer. As we've pointed out earlier, when it comes to a relationship between a man and a woman they are alike in a myriad of ways. Although, it may appear like men are from Mars and women are from Venus, there are similarities between the two planets. God wants to bring the two planets closer together as they follow Him down the road to oneness.

God wants us to depend on Him for answers and solutions in our relationships and our marriages. God wants us to be supportive, understanding and compassionate to the things that our spouses deal with on a day-to-day basis. This is impossible without conforming to His Word and His ways. If you want to make the world a better place open up your heart and let God make the change. Real change starts with accepting God into your life. God wants to change the man and woman that we see in the mirror to be more like His image. Real change comes from God.

Real Talk with Chris

I was born in Pittsburgh, Pennsylvania. When I turned nine years old, my mother moved my sister and I to Alexandria, Virginia. Not long after the move my mother got remarried.

As a child I remember my mother telling us, "as long as you live in this house, you are getting up on Sunday morning and to going to church." This was non-negotiable for her. I remember her playing her favorite Andre Crouch gospel record, "Soon and Very Soon" on Sunday's as we prepared for church.

After graduating high school, I went directly into the Marine Corps. I spent 13 of the toughest weeks of my life in boot camp in Paris Island, South Carolina. After graduating from boot camp, I had a mindset that I could accomplish anything that I set out to do. I was meritoriously promoted twice during my first tour of duty. After three years and four months of service, I was promoted to the rank of sergeant. I was determined to succeed.

My work ethic, drive and focus came from my mother. My charisma, wittiness and salesmanship came from my father. Interestingly, it was the women in my life that prayed for me and introduced me to my relationship with God. As a young man, I had my own personal relationship with God. In fact, I was a junior deacon in my childhood church Bethlehem Baptist Church in Alexandria, VA. I remember one of the deacons in the church, Frank Harvey, saying to my mother and I, "this young man has a major calling on his life—he is going to preach."

Unfortunately, at the time I didn't understand, nor was I ready to receive the gift and accept the assignment. I chose my own plan for my life and not God's plan. Like a lost sheep, I strayed from the shepherd. Growing up I never had any immediate family members who were ministers. I never witnessed what it was like for a man to lead his family to church or in prayer. My grandfather didn't go to church and my father wasn't around. My stepfather was the type of man who would give you the shirt off of his back but he went to church only because my mother required it.

I struggled as a child that my father was never there for me. I missed out on a lot of things that only a father can teach his son. I soon understood there was a difference between a "father" and a "daddy." The reality is that any man can be a part of making a baby, but it takes a real man to stay and be a daddy. A daddy is someone who is actively involved in his child's life on a daily basis.

My father was not a daddy because from the time of my birth, he was never around. It was tough for me to see other kids out on the football field playing catch and doing things with their dads. I am grateful for my stepfather who tried his best to step in and embrace me as his own son. However, for me there was still a void. The void was something that only the Heavenly Father could fill.

There were some things that the Marine Corps taught me that I never learned through any other male around me – honesty, integrity, dedication, and discipline... The Marine Corps helped make me into a stronger, more determined man, but my heavenly Father is responsible for making me into a better man. In fact, He's still working on me.

When I look at the man in the mirror, I see the shoulders of the men and the women that I stand on. I see the faces of family members who made sacrifice after sacrifice for me. I see the images of my mother and my father. I see the little boy who has grown into a man of character and substance. I see the shadows of my past. I see the man in the mirror that my father never could be. I see the scars of the man who had to overcome adversity. I see the man that my children need me to be. I see the man that the devil never wanted me to be. I see a man full of untapped potential. I see a man who knows his purpose. More importantly, the man that I see in the mirror is the man that GOD has created and called me to be.

However, as I look at the man in the mirror, I am mindful that I have to protect him from the voice inside my head. It is that voice inside my head that tries to distract me and interrupt me when I am focused and on the mission. It is that voice inside my head that says "yes" when I say "no." It is that voice inside my head that told me that I would never recover from losing my marriage, business and savings. It is that voice inside my head that wants to challenge the man in me by how much money I earn. However, I remind myself, that the God I serve is bigger than the voice in my head. The man in me is not defined or connected to the money in my pocket, the car that I drive or the house that I live in. There are no limits for the man in me when he connects with the God in me.

# Can We Talk?

Questions for you and your partner

The following questions will allow you to assess where you are on your journey to oneness with yourself and God.

1. What do you see when you see the man or woman in the mirror?

   _____

   _____

   _____

2. How do you feel about rejection? How do you react to it?

   _____

   _____

   _____

3. What is it that you struggle with daily?

   _____

   _____

   _____

4. What is it from your past that you are having a hard time letting go?

   _____

   _____

   _____

5. What is the voice that you keep hearing in your head? How do you deal with it?

   _____

   _____

   _____

6. What is it about your spouse that you appreciate the most?

_____

_____

_____

7. What are the examples that Christ modeled of a real man? How would you compare?

_____

_____

_____

8. I feel like my husband/wife doesn't understand me when...

_____

_____

_____

9. I believe God wants us to...

_____

_____

_____

Notes:

_____

_____

_____

_____

_____

9

What Are You Afraid Of?

O nce you accept Jesus Christ as your personal Savior you will begin going through a process of *conviction, conversion, and change.* Soon some of the things that you did in the past become difficult to do. This is because your conscious mind becomes *convicted* when you commit sin and then the Holy Spirit leads you to repent so that you can be free from guilt and shame. "When he comes, he will prove the world to be in the wrong about sin and righteousness and judgment" (John 16:8):

Trust

Vulnerability

Accountability

Transparency

GOD

Next comes the *conversion* phase. The process of conversion starts with belief, acceptance of God, faith in God, and repentance of your sins. Jesus answered, "I am the way and the truth and the life. No one comes to the Father except through me" (John 14:6 NIV).

After the conversion comes *change*. Change becomes apparent by the way you respond to situations that occur in your life. When you start to seek God through reading, studying, and applying His Word, change will be evident. Change will cause you to have a fresh outlook on life. Real change starts from within. God is the change agent. If you want change, you will find it in Christ. "Therefore, if anyone is in Christ, the new creation has come: The old has gone, the new is here" (2 Corinthians 5:17)!

If you want to witness the true manifestation of His power you will have to surrender your will to Him. For God to do new things in your life, there are some things that you must turn loose. Remember that change does not happen overnight. It doesn't come by waiving of a magic wand. Change comes when God takes the old you and births the new you in the spirit realm. This is when you have a spiritual encounter with God. You go from being lost in your sins to found in Him. John Newton wrote a song titled "*Amazing Grace*." One of the most famous lines is "I once was lost but now am found, was blind, but now I see."

When you decide to walk with Christ, you begin a new journey. Somewhere on that journey, God takes you through a progression of seasons that may not always feel good but they serve a purpose. As you seek to become more like Him, He will allow things to happen in your life that will develop your character. This is also known as pruning. God will continue pruning you as long as it takes for this is what will make you a stronger, more effective believer. "He cuts off every branch in me that bears no fruit, while every branch that does bear fruit he prunes so that it will be even more fruitful" (John 15:2). Just when you think you've arrived at the right address, He will call you to something new and higher. God wants to elevate your thinking, change your marriage and use you for His glory. To do this He must mold you like the potter with clay in His hands.

Once we accept Christ and become born again, we must ask God for grace to teach us how to completely TRUST Him. This is the hard part.

Trust

To trust is to believe with assurance in the ability, strength, and character of someone or something. Trusting in God requires us to live by faith. "Now faith is confidence in what we hope for and assurance about what we do not see" (Hebrews 11:1). Faith is a free gift from God. "For it is by grace you have been saved, through faith—and this is not from yourselves, it is the gift of God— not by works, so that no one can boast" (Ephesians 2:8–9). It is easy to talk about faith but very difficult to walk in faith.

Trusting in God means that you know God will honor His Word to help you overcome each test seen and unseen. When you trust God at His Word, you become empowered each time you read the scriptures to believe that God will fulfill His promises to you. "All Scripture is God-breathed and is useful for teaching, rebuking, correcting and training in righteousness, so that the servant of God may be thoroughly equipped for every good work" (2 Timothy 3:16–17).

When you trust God you not only take Him at His Word for your life, but for your marriage as well. The measure of our trust is evident to us when things go wrong and the waters get choppy. This is where your faith comes into play. However, it is not always easy to rely on faith to show up and save the day. The good news is the Bible gives us a recipe on how to make our faith active. James 2:14 asks the question, "What good is it, my brothers and sisters, if someone claims to have faith but has no deeds? Can such faith save them?" This means that faith without action is dead. You can believe God to save your marriage but you have to act like your marriage is worth saving for your faith to be effective. Pray and stand on God's Word. Then start making adjustments in your life to allow God to use you to be a blessing to your spouse.

As you adjust your attitude and your commitments to put God first and your marriage second, God will begin to move in your life. But remember, adjusting your life to God requires obedience, which will bring about growth. Growth can be painful. But if you want your marriage to grow, then you have to grow. Enlist people from a faith community (local church, ministry or faith–based organization) to help you grow as an individual before and after you say "I do." This is not the area of your life where you should chance going it on your own without the proper support. Scripture tells us to trust God. "For lack of guidance a nation falls, but victory is won through many advisers" (Proverbs 11:14).

In the average relationship, issues will arise unexpectedly. When this happens, it is common for the wife to rely on the husband and vice versa to discuss and resolve their issues. In most cases they have a dialogue with each other regarding the pros and cons before they make their choice. What happens if they do not agree? How do they get through it? Who do they trust? Oftentimes people put their trust in their spouses, when they know God's Word says not to put our trust in man, but we do it anyway. "It is better to take refuge in the Lord than to trust in humans" (Psalm 118:8).

Those who know your name trust in you, for you, Lord, have never forsaken those who seek you.

Psalm 9:10

Learning how to walk by faith is a process. All too often, because we do not see God we tend to put our trust in our spouses. They are there every day and we see them with our natural eyes. We grow dependent on them to provide, nurture and fulfill our desires and expectations. But there will be times when one fails to meet the other's expectations. This is where God wants you to trust Him to be your all and all.

God is Your Firewall

In the world of computers a firewall is built to prevent and protect the computer from malicious attacks or unwanted intrusions. A firewall separates a secure area from an unsecure area controlling communications between the two devices. There are multiple filters that send out communications back and forth. Each filter has its own role or works in tandem with another. The software firewall is typically found on a single computer or in small office networks that have broadband access. Its major function is to prevent unwanted access to the network by identifying high levels of vulnerability within risky ports.

Then there's the hardware filter, which is placed between two networks to separate less secure networks from secure networks. The hardware filter then helps create a hardware firewall that is designed to handle more complex issues. God is your hardware filter and the Bible is part of the firewall that protects you from dangers seen and unseen. When you have an ongoing, intimate relationship with Him, He is the filter that protects you from malicious attacks. He walks with you and talks with you through the voice of the Holy Spirit and the application of His Word. His purpose for your life is greater than what you can see.

It is human nature to come into a relationship bringing with you all the firewalls from your past hurts and previous relationships. Many times these issues are like cookies and cache that have never been deleted. What you'll soon discover is that no matter how hard you try to deal with them on your own, it just won't work. Each time you try to on your own you do more harm than good. You need God, who is the hardware filter, to step in and protect you. Allow Him to show His might and to cleanse you from all unrighteousness. Your firewall certainly does not have the capacity to do God's work. It's not strong enough, secure enough or complex enough to take on the issues of life.

When you try to take on God's role you become more susceptible to virus attacks from the enemy and other hidden dangers. God wants you to know that it's ok to put your TRUST in Him. God will resolve the situation. For you to trust God, you will have to completely turn your situations over to Him. This is where you will find yourself in a place of vulnerability. You won't have all the answers. You won't be able to solve the problems of your past and present. Rest assured God already knows your weaknesses and your shortcomings. Just know that you are vulnerable and prone to a higher level of malicious attacks without the right hardware filter – God.

As you walk with God and learn to trust Him, some people may not understand it. It is highly probable that you will be ridiculed, judged, condemned, and attacked. However, when you stand for God's purpose you are not worried about appealing to the masses. You are not worried about looking vulnerable to the eyes of man. You may not win a popularity contest, but your sole purpose is living your life pleasing to God.

Beware the enemy is always on the prowl. He wants to steal kill and destroy anything that he can. When given a chance he will penetrate your firewall and destroy your operating system. That's why he tries to attack your mind. If the devil can attack your mind by instilling fear, doubt and discouragement, then it will affect you in other areas. In your marriage, there are many scenarios where one or both parties are attacked at the same time.

The devil knows that if he can get through one of the protected firewalls the other firewall may become weaker. Therefore, you and your spouse must protect your system by running daily virus checks. One of the first virus checks to run in the morning is prayer and scripture reading. Although the attacks will continue to come, it helps to have a daily scriptural reference to ward them off. The Word of God is your sword. Use it so that you can win the battle for your mind on a daily basis.

Remember that your fight is not against your spouse, but against negative forces that try to destroy your marriage. Those forces can be described as spirits such as fear, anger, dishonesty, lust and so on. "For our struggle is not against flesh and blood, but against the rulers, against the authorities, against the powers of this dark world and against the spiritual forces of evil in the heavenly realms" (Ephesians 6:12). In a relationship, there are many trials that are designed to attack your inner spirit. The devil knows that if he can break your inner man he has a chance at destroying your trust in God. He wants to destroy the communication lines between you, your spouse and God. This is why both you and your spouse must have faith that is firmly rooted in God.

Many couples are in a very vulnerable place within their relationship. For example, you may be the communicator in your relationship and try to express your feelings with your spouse. Conversely, your spouse may withdraw when tough times come or avoid situations all together. These behaviors are not healthy and over time will become toxic to the chemistry of the relationship.

Even if the behaviors may occur infrequently, you both should address them before infrequent behaviors become the norm. Just know that your trust is not in man. Your trust is in God. Now is not the time to shut God out or push your partner away. Now is the time to trust God to see you through your situation. Your actions speak louder than your words. Sometimes your actions say that you are not completely willing to trust God and be vulnerable for His purpose. From now on make a commitment to activate your faith. Learn to trust God more than anyone or anything else. You will reap tangible and intangible rewards.

Vulnerability

Many of us are afraid to be vulnerable with another person. To be vulnerable means to be capable of being hurt or wounded. It can also mean feeling exposed. For most of us, we trust our spouses as far as we can see them. The moment something happens that reminds us of their failures or past mistakes, we regurgitate the same reactions. Then we find ourselves unwilling to let our spouses in. Some people are so tormented from past scars that they struggle being honest with their feelings. If this is you, I advise you to seek professional help to teach you how to overcome your challenges with trust. The foundation of your marriage is unstable if you don't trust your spouse with your feelings and God with your marriage.

Some people continue to deal with the same challenges long after the marriage vows have been exchanged. They continue to subdue certain feelings. In fact, they've covered up their feelings for so long that their partners are oblivious to any signs. One of the signs that a couple may have challenges in emotional intimacy and vulnerability is when they share secrets or thoughts with their closest friends that they would not dare share with their spouses.

It is human nature to hide signs of vulnerability. Many fear that their spouse will perceive them as weak, powerless or not in control. In a relationship both individuals want to appear to be strong, self-sufficient, independent and capable of handling any situation. For instance, a man will not likely ever say to his wife, "I am afraid." Being fearless, to a man, is a part of his role as a provider. Thus, the average man is afraid to be transparent and vulnerable especially with his wife. If her perception of his manhood is threatened in any way, and he knows it, his self-esteem will be severely affected.

Similarly, a woman doesn't want to have her womanhood questioned because of her potential shortcomings. She may never admit that she doesn't feel adequate enough to meet her man's needs. Moreover, she would never tell him that he is not a good lover or provider. She would rather keep it all in and figure out how to accept it. Not only is she afraid of sharing her true feelings for the fear of how he will react and accept it. She is genuinely concerned about his well-being and doesn't want to break down and destroy his manhood.

Men, just because you don't say "I'm afraid," her intuition will pick up on it if you remain silent. Moreover, you will leave her guessing about the problem and in some cases, she may think it's something that she has done. This is where she begins inquiring about your well-being...constantly. And the more she inquires, the more withdrawn you become. Do you see how the lack of true vulnerability can have severe consequences in a marriage? For both spouses, it can cause emasculation, lead to withdrawal, adultery, pornography and other forms of fulfillment.

Why are you afraid to be vulnerable within your relationship? Are you afraid to be authentic with your partner? If you can't be authentic with your partner who can you be authentic with? Do you feel that if you shared certain pieces of information with your partner they will hold it against you and perhaps judge you? There are many challenges that come up in life and you will need each other. When they do, you want the authentic partner to show up—not some imposter. When these challenges arise, managing them will require a source greater than you. It is important that you learn how to cast your cares on God. "Cast all your anxiety on him because he cares for you" (1 Peter 5:7).

Transparency

Transparency means to see through. Transparency in a relationship means to be honest and open with your thoughts and feelings

The diagram at the beginning of the chapter illustrates that when God is in the center of your relationship He will guide you on how to trust, be vulnerable, transparent and accountable within your relationship. As a couple, when you humble yourselves and seek His face together God will acknowledge your efforts. "Again, truly I tell you that if two of you on earth agree about anything they ask for, it will be done for them by my Father in heaven. For where two or three gather in my name, there am I with them" (Matthew 18:19–20).

If you are transparent with God, your walk with your partner will improve. Your ability to trust and communicate with each other will be enhanced. Being transparent not only requires honesty and openness, but a concerted effort from both parties to support one another and not be judgmental. Most couples want transparency, but never learn how to get there. They are too busy pursuing other things. Therefore, when God provides them with an opportunity to be transparent in their marriage, they miss it. When God sends a test He wants to teach you a lesson. If we miss God's intended message, we wind up repeating the test or suffering other consequences.

Transparency starts with YOU. You must learn how to be honest with yourself and then you can move towards transparency with your spouse. Being transparent with your spouse requires letting down your guard, removing the mask and accepting the things that you cannot change. Transparency involves sharing with your spouse even when it's not easy. "Therefore, confess your sins to each other and pray for each other so that you may be healed. The prayer of a righteous person is powerful and effective" (James 5:16). Transparency is about sharing the good, the bad and the indifferent. In your relationship it's about opening your mind and heart with your spouse. It's about sharing what's really going on.

Many couples wrestle with transparency when it comes to tough issues. They fear the truth will cause conflict. They find themselves at a place where they would rather sweep their issues under the rug. This is unhealthy. Not sharing your true feelings causes more harm than good. Bottled up emotions will eventually spill over and sometimes they create an overflow. It is better to share how you feel before things get to that point. Learning how to express your thoughts while considering the feelings of your spouse may seem challenging, but can be done.

The first step starts with you. Know that there is a time and season for everything. Not everything has to be addressed right when you think it should. "There is a time for everything, and a season for every activity under the heavens" (Ecclesiastes 3:1). Pray and ask God for the right time to speak to your spouse. Then ask God for the words to say. If you are afraid to approach your spouse, seek God for the strength that you need to be transparent with them. He will give you the courage to be open, honest and unashamed.

Any couple who has a healthy relationship will tell you that transparency is a two-way street.

Ultimately, they are seeking ways to build a healthy, lasting relationship. Their goal is to walk on the road of oneness together and within Christ. Couples that have a healthy relationship know that practicing transparency does not give them a pass to take off their gloves and use the "straight with no chaser" approach with their partner. They address each other in a respectful manner and show consideration to their partner's thoughts, feelings and concerns. They acknowledge that their relationship isn't perfect and that it takes hard work. They also accept that their relationship takes continuous commitment and effort. In fact, there are some days where they can't stand each other, but they acknowledge that it comes with the territory.

Transparency should not be used to manipulate or control your spouse. It's not about asking them twenty questions as if you are cross–examining a key witness during trial. Transparency in your relationship is about walking and trusting in God, submitting to His will for your lives. It's also about your willingness to be vulnerable in the flesh while walking in the spirit. Transparency becomes easier when you are simply not worried about pleasing the world. When it's all said and done, God is the one that determines your fate, people don't have a heaven or hell to put you in. Real intimacy within your relationship requires trust, vulnerability, transparency and accountability in God.

Accountability

Accountability means a willingness to accept responsibility for one's actions. Accountability has been a challenge long since the beginning of time. The Bible has shown us story after story of people not being responsible, but they were held accountable for the actions. The same holds true today. You are accountable for everything that you do and there are consequences for your actions.

Jonah disobeyed God's command for him to preach to the city of Nineveh. Jonah boarded a boat headed for another city instead of following God's instructions but God did not let Jonah off the hook. Jonah was thrown overboard by fellow passengers on the boat and then God sent a whale to swallow Jonah. Jonah remained in the belly of the whale for 3–days. He prayed, worshipped and repented there and God commanded the whale to release Jonah. The whale then vomited Jonah out on to dry land and finally, Jonah obeyed God's command to walk through Nineveh proclaiming that the city would be destroyed in 40–days if they didn't repent of their wicked ways. The Book of Jonah Chapter 3.

In the book of Exodus, God gave Moses the Ten Commandments because the people of Israel were worshipping idol gods and carrying on in their sinful ways. Like the Old Testament times, there are laws today that govern the land. If you break or violate these laws there are consequences to pay. You are held accountable for your actions. In marriage, God holds the husband accountable for the family because the man is the head. God's command to the husband is that he is to love his wife as Christ loved the church. " Husbands, love your wives, just as Christ loved the church and gave himself up for her to make her holy, cleansing her by the washing with water through the word, and to present her to himself as a radiant church, without stain or wrinkle or any other blemish, but holy and blameless" (Ephesians 5:25–27).

The challenge that we face today is that no one wants to be accountable for their actions. We all just want to live. We want to make the choices that we want to make. We want to enjoy living out a life of personal fulfillment, gluttony and sin with no strings attached. We don't want to accept responsibility for the consequences that result from our poor choices. The sins of the past are still the sins of today. The same struggles that Adam and Eve had are the same struggles that you and I have.

We can all agree that no one is perfect, but is that an excuse to continue to live a life of sin? When we accept Christ we ask Him to have reign and dominion over our mind and body. In fact, we openly profess that we accept His spirit. So then why do we continue to crucify Him over and over by sinful ways and poor choices? We all commit sin. However, God is looking for people today that will stand on the promise of His Word and not compromise His Word. His Word is full of instruction on how to gain wisdom and insight on this matter. Once we get it we must align with His Word.

Once you get in alignment with this concept you'll understand that accountability begins with being honest with yourself. Once you are willing to be honest with yourself then the reality is that you have to seek God.

God is a rewarder of those that diligently seek Him. "And without faith it is impossible to please God, because anyone who comes to him must believe that he exists and that he rewards those who earnestly seek him" (Hebrews 11:6). At the end of the day when the Book of Life is reviewed God will be the judge of our actions. We are accountable to Him. If God said it, then it's done. Why are you running away from God? What are you afraid of?

 # Real Talk with Chris

The older I get, the wiser I get and the more I learn to trust God. I wish I could say that I have always trusted God in every area of my life. The truth is that I have trusted Him in some areas, but not all. I am still growing. Even when I wrote this book I was still learning to trust God. I never went to college. I never wrote a dissertation and I had never written a book until now. In the words of my pastor, "I didn't graduate cum laude, magna cum laude, or summa cum laude. I graduated thank you Lord." While I do not have a degree, I believe that God can still use my gifts for His glory. Those who He calls He will also qualify. I believe that my experiences and life stories qualify me to share this message with you.

When I look back at my marriage I am thankful to God for His grace. As I said, in the introduction, divorce is not something that I would wish on my worst enemy. But I am grateful that God kept me through such a painful ordeal and did not allow the enemy to completely destroy my mind, will and emotions. I am grateful that my storm brought me closer to God.

I'll never forget the thoughts that the devil kept trying to feed me. "Where is your God now?" "Why isn't your God answering your prayers?" I recall attending noon day bible study class every Wednesday. I recall seeking spiritual prayer/accountability partners that would not just pray with me but hold me accountable for my actions. We prayed 3–days per week. I remember my mind racing in confusion. How could this be happening to me after I said, "Until DEATH do us part." I recall changing my music selection from secular to gospel.

My point is I did all of these things when I was going through, but I was not doing all those things consistently enough before the trial. Sure, I was a repeat Sunday Christian, but I wasn't actively in a ministry other than the monthly men's fellowship. I didn't seek God's face for every decision and for every plan that He had for my life. I was not willing to completely trust Him to guide and direct my steps. I was looking more at public perception and approval versus God's approval and plan for my life. I was afraid to be vulnerable and transparent with Him. Although, I thought I was praying and doing the right things that would draw me closer to God it wasn't enough. I really wasn't praying as often as I should have been when things were going well. God had some of me, but not all of me. Well, God got my attention. He knew just how to do it. Through the storm, God taught me the importance of praying, meditating, and fasting. "Do not be anxious about anything, but in every situation, by prayer and petition, with thanksgiving, present your requests to God" (Philippians 4:6).

 Can We Talk?

Questions for you and your partner

The following questions will allow you to assess where you are on your journey to oneness with yourself and God.

1. What are your challenges with trust?

   _____

   _____

   _____

2. What areas of your life do you not trust God with completely? How do you feel this has affected your relationship with God and your partner?

   _____

   _____

   _____

3. How would you define vulnerability?

   _____

   _____

   _____

4. Are you vulnerable in your relationship with God?

   _____

   _____

   _____

5. In what ways are you vulnerable in your relationship with your partner?

   _____

   _____

   _____

6. I need to... so that God can... (Complete the statement)

    _____

    _____

    _____

7. Transparency to me means... I am most transparent with my partner
    when it comes to...

    _____

    _____

    _____

8. Accountability to me means...

    _____

    _____

9. In what ways have you not been accountable to God and your part-
    ner? How can you make yourself accountable?

    _____

    _____

    _____

10. After reading this chapter, which of the four areas do you need to
    work on and why?

    _____

    _____

Notes:

    _____

    _____

    _____

    _____

10

If It Takes a Village to Raise a Child, Why Not a Marriage?

African villages are known to be family–oriented communities that adhere to particular customs and values that are unique to each specific village. Generally speaking, it is customary that the men teach the boys how to hunt for food and guard their homes. The women prepare the young ladies for motherhood and marriage. Together, the men and women work together to transfer certain values to their children so that a sense of cultural identity is preserved and passed on to the next generation. It is a scriptural mandate to instill values in the next generation. "Start children off on the way they should go, and even when they are old they will not turn from it" (Proverbs 22:6).

In western culture, we have seen a deterioration of the village. There is no longer a transfer of solid values from one generation to the next. What happened to the village? Have the elders stopped sharing the lessons of the past, concluding that times have changed so much that their values are no longer acceptable? Have we turned the keys to the village over to the children to raise themselves? Are the father and mother no longer in their rightful place as the heads of the village?

Everyone knows that raising children takes work. When a child is born it takes both parents, married or not, to assume responsibility for the child. Children need to see and experience unity and love within their village. The family is a child's immediate village and both parents need the support of other family members and friends to help raise a child. The village is much larger than just the mother and the father. The village is a support system designed to help raise the next generation to surpass the abilities and accomplishments of the previous generation.

Everyone plays a role in raising up the next generation of leaders. Raising children is a full-time job. From packing lunches to doing homework to disciplining and loving them, it takes more than just the two parents to do the job. It takes the help of family, clergy, neighbors and teachers to help raise a child. Unfortunately, many parents have mixed up priorities when it comes to raising children. Are we more interested in our favorite TV reality show than spending quality time with our children? Have we become a society that looks to teachers to raise our children? If so, we have missed the mark.

Times have changed and so have our values. A school principal could discipline a child for inappropriate behavior. Now, instead of correcting a child's behavior in school, schools suspend children for days and weeks at a time often resulting in failing grades for the child. Gone are the days when the parent could come up to the school and take disciplinary measures in their own hands. Now if a child comes to school and even says she or he was spanked, social services gets called into the home to investigate. Now, instead of spanking our children we may try to befriend them or we enable their behavior by making excuses for them and blaming the school system. The Bible tells us that the parent who loves his child will correct and discipline them. "Whoever spares the rod hates their children, but the one who loves their children is careful to discipline them" (Proverbs 13:24). An engaged parent does not parent from the sidelines. He or she is engaged with the child in the day to day hustle and bustle. It's not just about reading an announcement twice a year from the school newsletters. It's about getting involved with the development of your child socially and academically. You don't have to attend every PTA meeting to make a difference. Simply work with your spouse (if you have one) and your child's teachers, to make sure that his or her needs are being met. The more involved you are as a parent the greater chance that your child has of reaching their potential.

Unfortunately, so many parents have missed the mark because the village is no longer providing guidance for the family. Our values are centered less on God, family and education and more on money, self and significance. What we value has been transferred to our children. Thus, our children may be ambitious in certain endeavors but they lack the values that will keep them on the right path when they become adults. Bernie Madoff is an example of an ambitious and successful businessman who lacked the values to run an honest and legitimate business. His lack of values landed him a 150–year sentence.

What Happened to the Values In the Village?

There is a huge chasm in values between this generation and previous ones. The value system of those born during the Silent Generation era (1925–1945) was much different than the value system of those born during the Generation X era (1965–1981). Each generation faced different social and economic challenges. The Silent Generation was born during World War II. Many young men wanted to serve their country but were too young. This generation was considered to be very patriotic and self–sacrificing.

Generation X, on the other hand, was not big on patriotism, they were career driven. They were also exposed to high divorce rates and single-parent households. This era bore the world's first "latchkey" children. Kids at home alone while their parents were at work became the new normal. Many parents did not have a choice if they were single and could not afford child care. Thus, some kids learned to be responsible at an early age but many were left unattended and without guidance. Now, they are today's adults and we are only beginning to see the fruits of the generational transfer that they received. More kids in jail or having babies while still living at home. It is hard to watch this generation raise up another generation of children that lack the guidance they need to become the well-rounded leaders of tomorrow.

No matter what generation you are from, you have a responsibility to share information and pass on the values to each new generation. The moment that we stop sharing information is the moment that we stop growing. Although, each generation may face different socio-economic challenges, the values learned should not change. The last five generations have lost the values that were instilled in our parents, grandparents, and great-grandparents.

I was taught many important values that I try to pass down to my own children. Like sitting down and eating together as a family at the dining room table. Sharing stories as a family while gathered together in the living room. As a man I was taught to open doors for a woman or give up my seat to her. I remember my sister being taught to respect her elders and how to act like a lady.

These values were not only taught in the home, but they were reinforced outside the home. We were held accountable by the entire community. If a neighbor or fellow church member saw us acting inappropriately, they would correct us and then inform our parents immediately. Much like the African village, it was everyone's responsibility to raise the next generation. What values do you want to pass down to your children?

Who's Watching the Village?

A national park in South Africa had an overcrowded pen full of male bull elephants. To control the population, park management decided to move half of the baby population to another location. Soon after the move the park managers found dead rhinos in the park. Initially, they thought poachers were killing the rhinos, but that was ruled out because the tusks were still attached.

As it turned out, the baby bull elephants were killing the rhinos. When the park managers isolated them from their parents, they had no guidance. Therefore, the little bull elephants did what any child would do when no one was watching– run wild! The park management immediately transferred a few male bull elephants to watch over the young male bull elephants. This corrected the problem. By uniting the young bulls with older bulls, order was restored in the village.

The tendency of the baby bull elephant is much like that of our own youth. We hear of senseless killings and violence amongst youth. Without fathers or some other positive male presence, our children suffer. Men must teach young men how to act like men. While many women are forced to do it in some situations, this is not a woman's role. Being a father is a God–ordained role and men must take up the reigns in our families and communities.

Men have to provide a covering for the children and the family. Just because you don't have custodial rights or just because your father was not there for you does not give you a pass to put everything on the child's mother. Your children need you. They need the guidance and direction that only a father can provide. Don't let your relationship with the child's mother interfere with your relationship with your children. Someone has to continue to watch the village. "Fathers, do not exasperate your children; instead, bring them up in the training and instruction of the Lord" (Ephesians 6:4).

Ladies, if you are single, married or remarried and have children from a previous relationship, don't let the past relationship with the child's father influence the way you speak about him to the kids. And please, do not block him from spending time with his children. The children deserve to have a relationship with their father. Your objective should be to foster an environment that allows that to happen in spite of your feelings towards the father. I know this is not easy, but God will reward you.

No weapon forged against you will prevail, and you will refute every tongue that accuses you. This is the heritage of the servants of the Lord, and this is their vindication from me," declares the Lord.

Isaiah 54:17

But those who hope in the Lord will renew their strength. They will soar on wings like eagles; they will run and not grow weary, they will walk and not be faint.

Isaiah 40:31

If It Takes All This to Raise a Child, Why Not a Marriage?

If it takes a village to raise a child, then what do two adults need when they get married? When a child becomes an adult and decides to enter into the marriage covenant, it requires the support of the entire village. The village cannot just come to the wedding, eat the food and shirk off any responsibility to provide direction for the newly married couple. The village must be there to support and pray for this couple as they begin their lifelong journey.

Marriage is not a cake walk. The real work takes place after the ceremonial vows have been exchanged. Sometimes you will feel connected and sometimes you will not. Sometimes you will feel enamored with one another and sometimes you will not. That's where the village comes in. The village might be a family member, friend or fellow church member. Unfortunately, so many people keep things on the inside and never get help until it's too late. The most important tip that I can share is that it is best to get help early.

Too many marriages unravel when tested by the pressures of life. So many couples are overwhelmed by the day-to-day routines and need an outlet. They need someone that they can consult in their time of need. But many couples are afraid to open up to someone about what's going on in their marriage. Some people view counseling as failure. You have not failed by being proactive. You fail when you are reactive. No man or woman is an island all on their own. There's nothing wrong with attending a monthly couple's ministry or annual couple's retreat at your church. If you feel like you need to fellowship with other married couples, try finding a church with ministries exclusively for that purpose.

It is important to get replenished. Surround yourself with resources that can help strengthen and keep your marriage from getting disconnected. One of my favorite resources for couples and families is a ministry called Family Life. Family Life is a Christian-based organization focused on strengthening marriages and families. They have a host of resources from radio shows, magazines, books and events. I have utilized many of their resources and highly recommend them.

But we have this treasure in jars of clay to show that this all-surpassing power is from God and not from us. We are hard pressed on every side, but not crushed; perplexed, but not in despair; persecuted, but not abandoned; struck down, but not destroyed. We always carry around in our body the death of Jesus, so that the life of Jesus may also be revealed in our body. For we who are alive are always being given over to death for Jesus' sake, so that his life may also be revealed in our mortal body.

2 Corinthians 4:7–11

Find a couple that can share with you Godly principles and mentor you along your journey. It's one of the best things that you can do. There are a number of situations that will arise in your union. There will be circumstances that will come up where you'll want to give up and give in to the attack of the enemy. No matter how bleak the situation may appear, hang in there. This is where it will be helpful to know a few scriptures to help you overcome:

Notes from the Elders

Elder Bill and Deaconess Jenny Jones of my home church have been married for 48–years. They believe in living life with passion and zeal. Both in their 70's, they'll tell you that sex is better now than it has ever been. As I sought them for their thoughts on how to have a healthy, lasting relationship they shared a few pointers with me that I would like to share with you:

- Learn how to actively listen without preparing your rebuttal.
- Find out what the real problem is don't assume, be honest, direct, and focus on the issue at hand.
- Be careful with your body language. Your non–verbal language should match your verbal.
- Work hard to give each other pleasure and not pain.
- Check your motives – what's really behind the argument.

Are You Up For the Challenge?

In the NFL football is known as "the game of inches." The objective is to carry the football across the opposing team's goal. The defending team tries to block its opponent from touching its goal. Each team has several coaches who lay out a plan for them to execute for victory.

Marriage is like football. If your marriage is going to prosper it will take surrounding yourself with coaches (elders, like–minded couples, and other resources) that will support you in your walk towards a healthy and lasting marriage. These individuals are interested in your success. If you don't have anyone in your life who fills this role, pray and ask God to send someone into your life for this purpose. He will honor your request.

The sanctity of marriage is always taking a beating. From financial strain to the daily grind there is always something to threaten the peace in your home. This is why it takes a village to protect a marriage. In the village you never know who God will use to protect you from yourself and your opponent. On the football field if a player is not covering his position, the opponent can take advantage of this to gain ground. The same holds true for your marriage. If you are not watching your position, the enemy can step in and wreak havoc.

There will always be obstacles but continue to remain focused and cover your position. You and your spouse must be on one accord. You must commit to following God's word as the blueprint for your marriage. You cannot afford to allow any outside interference (e.g. impure thoughts, bad decision–making, meddling family members, etc.) to take you off course.

Although football has a winner and a loser your marriage does not. Use some of the tools shared in the previous chapters to work with your spouse. Your mission for the Kingdom is much too important. Don't let your unwillingness to yield to God's will lead you on a path to self–destruction. Use your village. It is there to help guide you and support you through your trials and tribulations. So, are you up for the challenge of being transparent and accountable to someone else? If not, then maybe you are not ready for marriage.

Real Talk with Chris

I exchanged wedding vows in front of hundreds of people. God kept a select few in my life for a reason. God selected certain people to be there for me during my highs and my lows. These people were my village.

When I needed a reality check, they gave it to me. When I needed a word of encouragement, they spoke into my life. These were the people God specifically ordained to be in my village. I had the choice to keep them out but I wanted to be accountable to someone. I wanted to be a better father and husband. Thus, I opened the doors of my village to whomever God sent my way.

I appreciate all of the men and women who were there to lift us up when I was down. I value those who celebrated with me when it was time to celebrate. I can't name all the names, but you know who you are. From the bottom of my heart, I thank you for your obedience and sacrifice.

Can We Talk?

Questions for you and your partner

The following questions will allow you to assess where you are on your journey to oneness with yourself and God.

1. What do you think happened to the village?

    _____

    _____

    _____

2. What role do you play in the village? In what ways can you help others?

    _____

    _____

    _____

3. If you have challenges in your relationship, who would you call?

    _____

    _____

    _____

4. How do you typically handle problems in your relationship? How does your spouse?

    _____

    _____

    _____

5. What values have you learned from previous generations? What values do you want to pass down to your children?

_____

_____

_____

6. In what areas have you caused pain in the lives of your children? What would you change?

_____

_____

_____

7. What are your beliefs when it comes to disciplining your children?

_____

_____

_____

8. What are your thoughts regarding raising children in a blended family?

_____

_____

_____

9. What are your thoughts regarding raising children in a bi-racial or bi-cultural family?

_____

_____

_____

10. I wish my mother/father had told me____. I wish my mother/father
    ____.

    _____

    _____

    _____

11. If you could change anything from your family history, what would
    you change?

    _____

    _____

    _____

Notes:

_____

_____

_____

_____

_____

Choose to LIVE
your life on PURPOSE,
not as a RESULT.

Chris Richardson

11

The Making of a Legacy

We all have a beginning and an ending to our lives. However, it's what you do in the middle that matters most. Everyone is given one life to live. You can choose to live your life in God's best or regretting that you never did. When it comes to your legacy, God has already written the script. He has ordained it from the beginning of time. Now, you must live by faith to let God accomplish His purpose through you.

When it's all said and done you can't change your past, but you can protect your future. Start by making different choices and choose to allow God to lead the way. Many times we get caught up in the "how" instead of the "who." God is the "who" that directs you towards having a promising future. When you choose to seek God, He will reward you for your obedience. "And without faith it is impossible to please God, because anyone who comes to him must believe that he exists and that he rewards those who earnestly seek him" (Hebrews 11:6).

Great leaders are known for the choices they make. They understand that in order to truly make an impact on the world, it requires surrounding themselves with the right people. For them to take their company from good to great it will involve making many tough decisions. Many companies will never realize what it means to leave a legacy because they aren't willing to put in the work required.

Many marriages will never leave a legacy for the same reason– they aren't willing to put in the work. The road to greatness requires a willingness to learn from past failures without dwelling on them. Life is full of ups and downs. But it's all about who you become through the experience on your journey towards greatness. Just because you made some mistakes early on in your life doesn't mean that your life is over.

The Winner in Me
Won't Let Me Quit

Now is not the time to give up on God. Could you imagine what life would be like if He gave up on you? It's never too late for God to turn your sadness into joy and your pain into your purpose. The only way that you lose is when you quit. Also, what you are running from might be the thing you should be running towards. In other words, the pain or struggle that you are trying to run away from could lead to the purpose God has planned for your life.

Senior PGA Professional, Michael Allen turned pro in 1984, at 25–years of age. He won the Scottish Open at the age of 30. But by no stretch of the imagination was his journey ever easy. He repeated Qualifying School 8–times. He played in over 334 professional starts without a win. Finally, frustrated with his results and concerned with his financial woes he called it quits on the game that he loved so much. As fate would have it, God used the hearts of other's to help sponsor his comeback. Twenty years later he won his first Senior PGA Championship. In his 50's he's playing the best golf of his life and is the leading money winner on the Senior PGA Tour. So what really changed for Michael Allen was his mental capacity. To win you can't quit.

In February 2007, Barack Hussein Obama would announce his candidacy for the 2008 Democratic presidential nomination. On January 20, 2009, he would be sworn in as the 44th President of the United States of America. In January 20, 2013, he would be sworn in for his second term in office. Not only was his legacy cemented in history as the first African–American President, but the first two–term African–American President. President Obama and First Lady Michelle Obama continue to live their dreams. They have encouraged and inspired millions with their story. Their continued acts of service and labor of love for God and country have demonstrated God's grace to mankind. Although, their journey is not complete they have truly left a mark.

Both of these men's stories are very different but from them we learn that passion, preparation and perseverance payoff. President Obama had a plan, surrounded himself with great talent and executed his vision. Both of these men had an encounter with their destiny. Both of them found their purpose through their struggles. Both of them had different outcomes. It can be said that life is not always what happens to you, but what you do with it. This same principle also applies to marriage.

When you get married, you will experience some good times and some bad times. You will experience tears of joy and tears of sadness, but don't quit storms don't lasts forever. If you are currently in a storm, just hold on and anchor your ship in Christ. There are some storms that will come with advance notice. So before it hits, stock your cabinets up with the supplies that you will need (faith, love, joy, peace). These are just a few items that you will need to help you live for today and be prepared for tomorrow.

Learn to see trials as opportunities to strengthen your walk with God and improve your character. The next time you encounter a challenge in your life or in your relationship, meditate on Philippians 3:14 and 4:13:

"I press on toward the goal to win the prize for which God has called me heavenward in Christ Jesus." "I can do all this through him who gives me strength."

He decreed statutes for Jacob and established the law in Israel, which he commanded our ancestors to teach their children, so the next generation would know them, even the children yet to be born, and they in turn would tell their children.

Psalm 78:5–6

What type of legacy will you leave behind?

Leaving a legacy is not always about leaving money or a business to your children. It is important to transfer certain values to your children that will teach them how to lead prosperous lives. You will not teach them this by giving them everything. Teach them from your mistakes. Make them work for their keep. Show them how good it feels to give back by taking them to a local homeless shelter or group home to volunteer. These memories are priceless and will pay tangible and intangible dividends for generations to come.

Real Talk with Chris

I remember taking a speaker boot camp offered by Willie Jolley. It was a 2–day training event on how to build your brand, get your message to market, and deliver proven results. I was the only trainee that had never written a book or delivered a presentation. In fact, I didn't even have a story. I always knew that one day I would empower and inspire others. What I didn't know was how or when God would show me the plan that He had orchestrated for my life.

The plan that He chose was not the path that I would have chosen for my life. That's why He is God. If it were up to me, I would have chosen to be some great real estate trainer. However, God had a different plan. He took the pain of a broken marriage and used it to show me my promise and lead me to my purpose. So, I promised Him that if He brought me out of my mess I would share my message of hope and love with the world. That tragic experience has brought me closer to Him. He has given me the ability to understand a woman's wants, needs, and desires and communicate that to other men. He has taught me how to love myself so that I can love others.

Along my journey my life has been full of little mini stories and blessings. My children have blessed me and helped shape me into a man of focus. For most men, becoming a father is a life–altering experience that makes us change some of our behaviors or ways of thinking. Because I have girls, I have no choice but to set a certain standard for the type of man I want them to bring home to me.

I've learned many lessons, but the most important lesson for me has been learning how to trust in God and let things go that I cannot control. God is teaching me how to have a healthy relationship with myself and with others. Life's lessons can sometimes knock you flat on your face, but in every lesson God reveals himself and teaches us how much we really need Him.

I am constantly reminding myself that God requires all of me (mind, body, spirit) to be focused on Him. God wants to have an intimate relationship with me when things are good and bad. Although my journey is not complete the one thing that I am confident of is that I have become a better man, and father as a result of my experiences. I am working on the middle of my life story and I will leave a lasting legacy for my children and their children.

Here's what I believe: you can't control the beginning and you can't control the ending, but you sure can work on the middle. I am now working on the middle of my story. Everyday there are successes and failures. I may have failed in one area or another in my life, but my failure does not make me a FAILURE. I've learned to call on the name of Jesus before the storm, in the midst of my storm and after the storm. I've learned that my trials are a test to grow my character and increase my walk with Him. I have learned how to thank Him in advance even when I can't see how the story will end.

Overall, I have learned that life can sometimes squeeze the JUICE out of you. In fact, life can squeeze you to the point where you want to cry or give up. Life can leave you with no other choice but to produce something positive out of your negative experiences. Life will either make you bitter or BETTER. It all depends on your attitude. Just remember that while you're working on your legacy some of your greatest potential has yet to be released. Sometimes God has to wait to the right season to release it. Some of you are pregnant with purpose. It's time to give birth. It's time to P.R.O.D.U.C.E.

P   Pray and push towards your destiny
until something happens.

R   Rethink your strategy. You're
going to need one.

O   Observe your surroundings. Everything
and everybody may not be your friend.

D   Decide the best approach to
handle the situation.

U   Be unwavering in your commitment to
God's plan for your life.

C   Conquer any distractions
before they conquer you.

E   Elevation comes from God, not man. So, in all your ways
acknowledge Him and He shall direct your path.

Remember there's a purpose inside of you waiting to be birthed,

Can We Talk?

Questions for you and your partner

The following questions will allow you assess where you are on your journey to oneness with yourself and God.

1. 50 years from now what do you want your children to tell their children about you?

   _____

   _____

   _____

2. When the eulogy is read and the casket is closed. What phrase would be inscribed on your tombstone?

   _____

   _____

   _____

3. What would you buy if money were endless?

   _____

   _____

   _____

4. Life to me is about _. Marriage is about ___. Family is about___.

   _____

   _____

   _____

5. I need to change____ so that I can ____.

_____

_____

_____

6. I am learning how to____.

_____

_____

_____

7. I need to surround myself with people who _.

_____

_____

_____

8. I see my spouse and I doing __ in the future.

_____

_____

_____

Notes:

_____

_____

_____

_____

_____

When you are old and looking back over your life, what is the legacy you want to leave behind? What do you want to teach your children, grandchildren and great–grandchildren?

What is your story?

Complete the following. This is my story...

*Only what you do for
Christ
will last forever.*

Larry Parrish

Made in the USA
San Bernardino, CA
10 February 2014